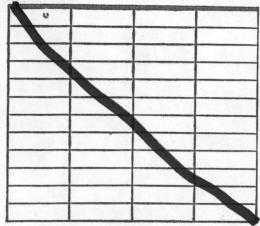

SMALLER IS BETTER

SMALLER
IS
BETTER

Japan's Mastery of the Miniature

O-Young Lee

translated by Robert N. Huey

KODANSHA INTERNATIONAL
Tokyo, New York, and San Francisco

With the exception of the title page, all Chinese, Korean, and Japanese names in this book are given in traditional order, with surname first.

Originally published under the title *Chijimi shikō no Nihonjin* by Gakuseisha, 1982.

Distributed in the United States by Kodansha International/USA Ltd., through Harper & Row, Publishers, Inc., 10 East 53rd Street, New York, New York 10022. Published by Kodansha International Ltd., 12-21, Otowa 2-chome, Bunkyo-ku, Tokyo 112 and Kodansha International/USA Ltd., with offices at 10 East 53rd Street, New York, New York 10022 and The Hearst Building, 5 Third Street, Suite 430, San Francisco, California 94103.

First English edition, 1984.

Library of Congress Cataloging in Publication Data
Yi, O-nyŏng, 1934–
   Smaller is better.
   Translation of: Chijimi shikō no Nihonjin.
   1. National characteristics, Japanese. 2. Japan—
Civilization. I. Title.
DS830.Y513   1984   952   83-48883
ISBN 0-87011-654-1
ISBN 4-7700-1154-7 (in Japan)

CONTENTS

1. The Naked Truth about Interpretations of Japan   9
   A Festival of Interpretations of Japan   9
   Forks and Chopsticks   13
   Little Giants   18
   Haiku and Mame-emon   20

2. Smaller is Better: Six Examples   25
   Boxes within Boxes—The Principle of Inclusion   25
   The Fan—Fold It, Hold It, Bring It Closer   31
   The *Anesama* Doll—Take Away and Pare Down   40
   The Well-stuffed Box Lunch—Pack It In   47
   The Nō Mask—Assuming a Proper Attitude   53
   Family Crests—Congealing   62

3. The Culture of Reductionism
   as Manifested in Nature   72
   Ropes and Wheels   72
   The Garden as Picture Scroll   77
   Dry Landscape—The Beautiful Captive   82
   Bonsai—Delicate Chamber Music   87
   Ikebana—Cosmic Flower Petals   91
   The God on the Ceremonial Shelf
       and the Urban Recluse   96

4. Reductionism as Found in People and Society   111
   Understanding the Four-and-a-half-mat Space 111
   The Tension Culture 118
   One Meeting in a Lifetime 126
   The Concept of the Theater 135
   The *Hanamichi* in Modern Society 144
   Assembling Things 147

5. Reductionism Today   153
   Transistors Reflecting the Japanese Spirit 153
   Reductionism and Management 157
   The Robot and *Pachinko* 161
   Speculation and Innovation 165

6. Expansionism and the Japan of Today   170
   Pulling in Other Lands 170
   The Samurai Merchant 176
   A Fear of Open Spaces 179
   The Handtruck and the Raft 183
   Ah, To Be an Honorary White Man! 184

Conclusion: Don't Become Demons,
            Become Issun Bōshis! 187

Index 190

All things small,
no matter what they are,
all things small are beautiful.

Sei Shōnagon
The Pillow Book

1

THE NAKED TRUTH ABOUT INTERPRETATIONS OF JAPAN

A Festival of Interpretations of Japan

I am not here to write about Japan from the standpoint of some university professor, hair streaked with gray. Nor am I writing as a cultural critic, nearsightedly squinting through his glasses. I see things, instead, through the eyes of one who got his first look at Japanese culture when he was a boy at elementary school.

The shelves in my study are packed with books, more of them on Japan than on any other subject. But I would rather leave those aside and approach this work with a small white notebook and a tiny stub of a pencil taken out of the satchel slung over my schoolboy shoulders. Nor must I forget perhaps the most important thing: a soft and efficient eraser.

I am not just being allusive or allegorical. I did indeed learn my Japanese and most of what I know about Japan in the classroom of an elementary school before the end of the Second World War, while Korea was still a Japanese colony. But why would I want to go back to a time when my Japanese language skills were meager and my ideas unformed—to the days of my youth—in order to talk about Japan?

I was inspired in my audacious move by the well-known Andersen fairy tale *The Emperor's New Clothes*. The adults in that story conjured up illusory clothes for the emperor. Even if some of them noticed that he was actually naked, they said nothing, preferring to think that they themselves were seeing wrong. The eyes that discovered that the emperor had not a stitch on were those of a child. And the only voice that proclaimed this discovery was a child's voice.

Many of the countless books that have been written about Japan have been showy, like French fashion magazines, and popular because of that. Since the end of the war alone, there have been innumerable interpretive works written about Japan. Some of them, such as Ruth Benedict's *The Chrysanthemum and the Sword*, *The Anatomy of Dependence* by Doi Takeo, and *Japanese Society* by Nakane Chie, have contributed new words to the popular vocabulary. Others, particularly Japanese books, have taken their titles from such phrases already in popular use as "economic animal" and "Japan Inc." In Japan these interpretations of Japanese society inevitably become best sellers, and large numbers of people pick up the jargon in them just as they would pick up and carry the portable shrine at a local festival. Such jargon appears in newspaper headlines, in magazine editorials, in talks given by television and radio commentators. In the hands of writers with more artistic inclinations, this vocabulary that began in the halls of academia ends up as words to a popular ballad.

This festival of interpretations makes it all but impossible to see the real, the naked Japan with one's own eyes. Before one knows it, that naked Japan is dressed in illusory clothing by the masses and pop culture. That is why I decided here to examine Japanese culture through the eyes of an elementary school child.

Why should it be that interpretations of Japan, whether they be by Japanese or Westerners, are cloaked in this illusory clothing? And what is the nature of the child's vision that could expose this cover-up? *The Anatomy of Dependence*, one of the most widely known interpretations of Japan, provides some clues. It is typical of the genre. I am particularly interested in this book, not so much because of its content but because of its attempt to discover what is unique about the Japanese psychology and because of the way its author, Doi Takeo, makes his case.

Doi states his methodology quite clearly: "If there is anything unique about the Japanese psychology it must be closely related with the uniqueness of the Japanese language." And Doi hits upon the concept of *amae* (dependence) and is convinced of "the uniqueness of the word *amae* as an item of vocabulary in Japanese." But is "dependence" as Doi defines it peculiar to the Japanese language? For if it is not, his whole argument goes up in smoke. And indeed, it is not.

The fact is that in Japan's nearest neighbor the concept of "dependence" is as common as pebbles scattered by the roadside. In Korean, there are two equivalent terms for the Japanese word *amae*: *ŏrigwan* and *ŭnsŏk*. Both are an integral part of daily speech. Not only are there equivalent words, but the concept of dependence plays such a crucial role in child rearing in Korea that one could say dependence is even more inextricably bound up with the Korean psyche than it is with the Japanese. Such Korean words as *ŏmsal*, used to gain the sympathy of others by exaggerating one's pain and suffering, are far more complex than the simple Japanese term *amae*.

This being the case, why did a learned scholar like Professor Doi make such a grave error by asserting that the concept of dependence as expressed by the term *amae* is peculiar to Japan? The problem is not Professor Doi's alone. His argument is merely the product of a sense of separateness from the rest of Asia, a feeling that the Japanese have entertained ever since the Meiji Restoration of 1868. Professor Doi relates that what convinced him *amae* was a word peculiar to the Japanese language was a conversation he once had with a British woman who spoke fluent Japanese. She was talking in English about her child's infant years but suddenly switched to Japanese to say, *"Kono ko wa amari amaemasen deshita"* (We were not especially indulgent with this child). When Professor Doi asked her why she had used Japanese only for that one sentence, she replied that there was no way to say such a thing in English.

From this Doi adduces that *amae* is a word unique to the Japanese language. It is a strange leap of logic, and it is an indication of just how deeply the Japanese have come to believe, since the Meiji Restoration, that English is *the* language of the West, and even of all the rest of the world. How else could Doi have been led to believe that if a Japanese word does not exist in equivalent form in English it must be peculiar to Japanese? Perhaps this is the key to the "illusory clothes" that cloak Japan and interpretations of Japan.

This sort of premise, that if it does not exist in English it must be peculiar to Japanese, is not uncommon. Many interpretations of Japan written by Japanese revolve around just such simple Japan versus Britain/America comparisons. Even those works that take a somewhat wider view broaden only one side of the equation, substituting Westerners for British and Americans. Although we can imagine Doi substituting a French or German mother in his story, would he have ever considered a Korean woman? Yet if one is trying to find out whether or not *amae* is a uniquely Japanese concept it seems that a normal first step would be to look at a language such as Korean, which has a much closer linguistic relationship to Japanese than do any of the European languages.

This reluctance among Japanese writers to "look East" is far from uncommon. As a result, they often call something uniquely Japanese when it would be more relevant to call it common to Japan and Korea, or to all of East Asia. We need not go far to find examples. The popular historian Higuchi Kiyosuke has written, "Among the civilized countries of the world Japan is the only one where seaweed is eaten." But he has apparently forgotten that Korea is a major producer and consumer of seaweed. In the book *Nihonjin no kokoro* (*The Spirit of the Japanese*) by Umesao Tadao and four other Japanese scholars, it is boldly asserted: "The realization that night soil, human excrement, could be used as an organic fertilizer for vegetables was an amazing discovery." Umesao and his fellow authors conclude that it was originally a Japanese idea, failing to recognize that other people have long made use of this "high-level agricultural technology" (to use their own words). Anyone could tell after a few minutes in a Korean village that this wonderful organic technology is hardly unique to Japan.

This is the same kind of short-cut logic we find in the *amae* argument: if it does not exist in the West, it must be peculiar to Japan. I have no desire to enter into a debate here on Japan's claim to the dubious distinction of a monopoly on *amae*, much less night soil. Nor do I seek to refute the work of these scholars. What I wish to point out is that sometimes popular books interpreting Japan, be they by Japanese or foreigners, wrap Japanese society in illusory clothing that bears little relation to reality. And this is usually because the basis of such books is a comparison only between Japan and the West.

The counterpoint to Western culture is not simply Japanese culture. Asian culture, although it does include Japan, is not defined merely by the experience of that one people. Characteristics of European culture must be seen in relation to all of Asia, not just Japan. For if we compare Japan only to the West, we run the risk of jumping to the mistaken conclusion that something is peculiar to Japan when in fact it might well be common to the entire Northeast Asian cultural sphere.

Forks and Chopsticks

China and Korea, both of which have histories longer than Japan's, receive scant attention in books of cultural comparison. To be sure, there are Japanese scholars specializing in Japanese culture who realize that to understand the roots of Japanese history one must study ancient Korean history and language. But the majority of those who write interpretations of Japan cannot break free of the parochial outlook that is exemplified by the implicit use of the West as a standard.

This same problem exists in the works of Westerners writing about Japan. Imagine for the moment a Westerner who, knowing nothing about China or Korea, observes Japanese eating habits for the first time. He sees that Japanese eat with chopsticks rather than a fork, that they eat rice instead of bread, and that they eat from a bowl rather than from a plate. Will he not attribute these practices exclusively to Japan?

In fact, this is more or less what we find in an interpretation of Japan written by the famous European thinker Roland Barthes. In his *L'Empire des signes* he writes that "the sole element that gives Japanese cooking its value" is "rice boiled until it is sticky yet still loose and dry." He goes on to say that "this boiled rice, . . . which is really separate particles congealed into a soft mass, . . . can be broken apart with just one thrust of the two chopsticks." These chopsticks, Barthes asserts, are, along with the rice, specifically Japanese things.

Now what if a non-European, a Korean, takes a look at Japanese eating habits? He sees nothing at all unusual about the fact that rice is eaten or that chopsticks are used. The only thing that he notices about Japanese eating customs is that people eat their rice in small bowls, which they fill again and again. Thus, to the Korean, what is peculiar to Japan at meal times is that people eat rice out of little bowls, not the fact itself of eating rice or using chopsticks. The Korean thus reveals a more subtle understanding of what is unique about Japan than the European.

But what if the Japanese, knowing full well Western eating habits, did not realize that Koreans and Chinese eat rice with chopsticks, or indeed that they originated the custom? They would assume, as Europeans do, that eating rice with chopsticks is unique to Japan. Some Japanese writers appear to make equivalent assumptions. They know that English has no word for *amae* but do not realize that Korean has many. Japan is a nation where Lincoln and Kant are widely studied but King Sejong and the Confucianist Yi Hwang are virtually unheard of.

So it is that the Japanese seem incapable of examining their own culture through comparison with that of Korea, even though Korean language, customs, and culture, unlike those of Europe, have much in common with Japan, and despite Korea's profound impact on the development of Japanese culture.

The Portuguese Missionary Luis Frois, writing in the sixteenth century, examined the customs of Japanese children. Of the twenty-four traits he listed as characteristic of Japanese youngsters, only five or six are actually unique to Japan. For example, the use of chopsticks, the learning of reading before writing, and the carrying of babies strapped to their backs by young girls are all common to Korea as well as Japan. Frois, who knew nothing about Korean customs, relied solely on his observations, and had no way of knowing which of the traits he saw were truly unique to Japan. Frois's approach resurfaces in the work of Ruth Benedict. In her book *The Chrysanthemum and the Sword*, many of the qualities Benedict identifies as peculiar to Japan, such as the sense of debt and loyalty (*giri ninjō*), the sense of shame (*haji*), and certain child-rearing practices, are actually Confucian in origin and characteristic of Korea as well.

Books like *The Anatomy of Dependence* and *Japanese Society* are products of a Japan that knows little about Korea and has forgotten the historic influence Korea has had on its neighbor. For example, much is made in *Japanese Society* of the use of polite language (*keigo*) in Japanese for distinguishing between people of various status levels. But this is something that has its linguistic roots, and modern parallels, in Korea. Indeed, the use of polite language is far more subtle and complex in Korean than it is in Japanese.

If the Japanese made a careful study of Korea rather than the West they would probably write that Japanese society shows a strong horizontal rather than vertical emphasis. They would see, for example, that in traditional Korean villages there was never anything equivalent to the communal house where young people would gather in the evening that was once a part of Japanese rural life. If Professor Doi had known Korean, he might not have chosen *amae* as the unique Japanese word on which to base his theories. Rather, he might have noted how different such Japanese terms as *daijōbu* (everything's alright) and *hadaka ikkan* (starting from scratch), both of which emphasize independence not dependence, are from anything found in Korean. Although the Chinese characters used to write these two terms are recognizable to Koreans, they carry none of the connotations in Korea that have been given them by the Japanese.

Japan shares with China and Korea the use of Chinese characters for writing. The three countries also share religious tendencies, emphasizing Confucianism, Buddhism, and the worship of local gods. Furthermore, they are all rice-growing societies. Why is it, then, that only Japan has been able to modernize? Why has Japan alone among the nations of Asia managed to industrialize to a level on a par with the West? This is the kind of question a Westerner might ask. The issue thus becomes not how Japan is different from the West but how it is different from the rest of East Asia. Seen in this light, things at first thought to be uniquely Japanese in fact turn out to be characteristic of China and Korea as well.

Similarly, the Korean view often brings a fresh perspective to what are by now familiar Western reactions to Japanese culture. When, for example, a visiting American poet saw the staggered stepping-stones leading to the entrance of a tea room, he praised the Japanese as being, in all the world, the people most appreciative of the beauty of nature. He noted that, unlike Westerners, who would make the route from the outer gate to the house as straight and short as possible, the Japanese created a meandering, nonfunctional path so that the garden could be appreciated from various angles. But to a Korean, these staggered Japanese stepping-stones are the very antithesis of nature. They are artificial, even mechanical. To the Korean, who seeks to merge with nature, the very act of laying a path of man-made stepping-stones seems unnatural. To limit beforehand, by means of stepping-stones, the natural human gait seems a kind of tyranny. Perhaps to an American poet, raised in a culture that prizes man-made artificiality as symbolized by the straight line, the Japanese staggered stepping-stones appear to represent a love of nature. But to a Korean poet, brought up in a culture that holds that a path should open up naturally before one as one walks along it, these stepping-stones seem contrived.

To the extent that the Japanese overlook, or are ignorant of, Korea, they are hurting themselves more than they are doing an injustice to Korea. So often, ignorance of Korea prevents a full understanding of Japan. Like a sunflower turning its face to the sun of European culture, a writer about Japan runs the risk of being blinded and unable to see the emperor without his clothes.

Now let me explain why I have turned to writing an interpretation of Japan. As a child of eight in a school classroom, I had direct experience of Japanese culture, a culture whose characteristics on the surface seemed similar to those of my own but which I instinctively felt were somehow different. In that colonial classroom with its Rising Sun flag and its portrait of the Japanese General Nogi, I was taught that Japanese and Koreans were one and the same and therefore spent my youth without any particular consciousness of what it meant to be a Korean. Yet at the same time a part of me was firmly convinced that I would never be able to assimilate fully into this Japanese culture that was being forced upon me.

I feel that if I write from this standpoint—as one who grew up without a strong sense of racial or cultural identity yet knew that there was somehow a gap between himself and the situation he found himself in—my view might be like that of the child in the Andersen fairy tale.

Little Giants

How does a child see Japan, a child struggling to learn reading and writing in a gray colonial classroom in occupied Korea? Being a child, perhaps he would associate the thought of Japan with Morinaga caramels or Japanese King crayons. But these everyday items constitute a general sort of childhood memory not specifically associated with Japan.

The first Japanese I ever "met" was not General Nogi, whose portrait hung in our classroom. Nor was it our balding school principal, who each morning would lead us in the pledge of allegiance to Japan. No, strangely enough the first Japanese I remember are the characters I met in fairy tales: Issun Bōshi, Momotarō, Kintarō, and Ushiwakamaru. And the clearest impression I have of them is that they were all little giants. In their imaginary world a needle became a sword, a bowl became a boat, with chopsticks for oars. The slightest breath was a typhoon; the tiniest ripple became a tidal wave. Yet in this world Issun Bōshi, tiny as he was, was no weakling, no meal for a hungry frog. Precisely because he was small, he could go undetected by the largest of demons and turn around and capture them. Like Momotarō, he was a little giant who subdued much larger foes and returned home with a treasure to show for it.

In Korean folklore there are no heroes like this. Among the tales handed down for centuries in the thick dialect of the countryside, there are many about simple countryfolk who outwit their cleverer foes or who defeat demons in battle. But there are no stories about dwarfs or children defeating giants. Fantastically tiny creatures like Issun Bōshi simply do not appear in traditional Korean stories. In fact, strictly speaking, there is no word for dwarf in the Korean language. The typical heroes of Korean folk tales are giants. The Korean folk tale counterpart of Issun Bōshi, the tiny priest with an outsized head and a body that tapers downward and who gets smaller each time he is struck, is a monster egg that grows larger the more it is hit.

A closer examination reveals that the differences between Korea and Japan in attitude toward size are not confined to folklore. In Korean, for instance, although there is a prefix denoting enormity, there is none to indicate diminution. The Korean prefix *wang*, when added to a word, shows that the object is much larger than ordinary. It functions like the "king" in the English expression "king-size" and in fact has the same original meaning. Even Japanese tourists who spend just a short time in Korea quickly learn the expressions *wangdaep'o* (king-sized bowl), *wangnun* (king-sized eyes), and *wangbŏl* (king-sized hornet) in the local drinking establishments.

In Japanese, however, it is not the prefixes for "huge" but those for "tiny" that are commonly used. There is the prefix *hina* (literally, "chick"), for example, or the much-favored *mame* (bean—used in a way similar to the "pea" in "pea brain"). The round *mame* (bean) is like a condensed representation of the world. Whatever this prefix is attached to suddenly shrinks in size to fit Issun Bōshi's world. Issun Bōshi himself is also referred to by the names Mametarō and Mamesuke (*tarō* and *suke* being traditional components of Japanese boys' names). Similarly, such words as *mame-bon* (mini book), *mame-jidōsha* (mini car), *mame-ningyō* (mini doll), and *mame-zara* (mini plate) all denote objects that are much smaller than normal.

When I was a child, the things we recognized as Japanese rather than as part of our own culture—be they in the imaginary world of fairy tales, in the realm of language, or even everyday objects—invariably bore the stamp of Issun Bōshi. If one explores this concept of miniaturization beyond Japanese folklore into other aspects of Japanese culture, one discovers fascinating realms—of tiny festival dolls, for example, and dwarf trees. And here one gets a glimpse of what is unique in Japanese culture.

In Japanese, the generic word for "craftsmanship," *saiku*, translates literally as "delicate workmanship." In other words, to craft something is to make it smaller and fashion it delicately.

And besides, the prefix *ko* (small) can be attached to form the word *kozaiku*, "small, delicate workmanship." Conversely, something which is large and ungainly is called *busaiku* (not delicately crafted). In Japan things that have been reduced in scale and minutely crafted are not merely miniatures. They are more charming and more powerful than their larger counterparts, and there is something of a mysterious aura to them.

As a child, I was deeply impressed by the Japanese tendency to contract things rather than expand them. It seemed to me that the everyday articles used by the Japanese were about one-third the size of those used by us Koreans. Japanese rice bowls, cushions, trays, saké cups, and fans were all smaller than their Korean counterparts.

Many people turn to superficial geographical determinism to explain the Japanese tendency to make things smaller. They point out that Japan is, after all, an island country. Yet it was not until Japan opened itself up to the West in the second half of the nineteenth century that the idea caught on of Japan as an island country. The first use of the term "island country personality" is generally credited to the historian Kume Kunitake, who employed the phrase after returning to Japan from his travels in Europe during the Meiji era (1868–1912).

Small and mountainous though Japan may be, however, it is still more spacious than Korea, and as for "island country consciousness," this has not stopped Britain, once ruler of the seven seas, from showing a marked tendency toward expansion rather than contraction. In other words, it seems quite plausible to argue that it is not so much Japan's external conditions that drove it toward smallness as an innate propensity toward shrinking things.

Haiku and Mame-emon

It should come as little surprise to learn that Japan possesses the world's shortest poetic form, the *haiku*. The *haiku* is just one-third as long as Korea's shortest verse form, the *sijo*. But its very brevity enabled the poet Kobayashi Issa (1763–1827) to use it to write of the complexities of human existence and the inexorable movement of time by the faint light from the tiny lamp wick next to his pillow. *Haiku*, which give expression to the vastness of space and time in just seventeen syllables, are the text for the study of Japan's tendency to make things smaller.

The uniqueness of *haiku* lies not only in their brevity. They represent a special aesthetic that reduces our great, wide, vague world into a small, manageable form. A fine example of this is one of Issa's *haiku*:

How beautiful!
Through a hole in the paper screen
I see the Milky Way.

Although it is true that Issa was bedridden at the time he wrote this poem and could not therefore have moved around even if he had wanted to, it is also clear that he had no great interest in going outside and looking at the vast night sky. Rather, it was a glimpse of the Milky Way through a small tear in the paper screen window that moved him to write the verse.

Just as they found prodigious strength in little Issun Bōshi, the Japanese discovered a special beauty in small, finely detailed things. In the *Man'yōshū*, Japan's earliest poetry collection, compiled in 759, the flower most often mentioned (it appears in 141 poems) is the bush clover, but it is rarely mentioned in Chinese and Korean poetry. Unlike those of the peony, the favorite of Chinese poets, bush clover blossoms are small and grow in dense clusters, according well with the other autumn grasses and flowers loved by the Japanese. Cherry blossoms; lilies of the valley, emblems on the stationery of countless college coeds; and wisteria, the most popular of names for bars and coffee shops in Tokyo—all of these, like the bush clover, have tiny, delicately shaped flowers.

A look at the etymology of the Japanese word for "beauty" reveals that the concept of beauty has always been associated by the Japanese with small, delicately wrought things. Before the Heian period, in the eighth century and before, the word that now means "beautiful," *utsukushi*, had the connotation of "love." This was the way it was used in the eighth-century history, the *Kojiki* (*Record of Ancient Matters*), for example. When the early writers wanted to call something beautiful, they used the word that now means "detailed," *kuwashi*; thus a "detailed woman" was one who possessed a wondrous beauty.

In his book *Tōyō bigaku* (*East Asian Aesthetics*), Imamichi Tomonobu says that the adjective *meguwashi* (literally, "detailed to the eye") was used to describe a fine, crystalline scene. He adds: "There is no doubt that the word detailed [*kuwashi*] was applied to things that had achieved a minutely detailed, completed state. The term 'detailed things' [*kuwashi-mono*] referred either to objects to which human workmanship had been applied or to people of refinement. In either case it was implicit that the object had been fully realized."

Ōno Susumu, in interpreting a long poem from the *Man'yō-shū* (chapter 13, no. 3331), discusses the phrase "the mountain is detailed" (*yama no kuwashi*) as follows: "The trees are densely packed on the mountainside, so densely packed that the harder one looks the harder it is to see any space between them. This is what is meant by 'the mountain is detailed,' and it certainly implies beauty."

Following this logic we would be safe in calling bush clover, wisteria, and cherry blossoms "detailed flowers." To the Japanese, things beautiful are things that show minute detail, things that are small and crystallized into dense clusters.

The same phenomenon can be seen in Japanese fiction, where the novel gives way to the short story and the short story yields to the sketch. Although it was short-lived, there was a movement in the mid 1920s, led by the writers Okada Saburō and

Takeno Tōsuke, that advocated ultrashort stories of just two or three pages. And the Nobel Prize–winning writer Kawabata Yasunari wrote more than a hundred short sketches in his lifetime.

In contrast to the short stories and dwarf heroes of Japan, there is, it seems to me, a certain European ideal embodied in Rabelais's *Gargantua*. In Gargantua, who drank the milk from 12,913 cows at one sitting and whose underwear required a thousand meters of cloth, we can see the aspirations of Renaissance Europeans, who wanted to become "giants." In this giant, who used the bells of Notre Dame as trappings for his horse, they heard the call toward a new and greater human existence, one that challenged them to become self-confident and strong.

"Ever larger! Ever larger!"—at about the same time Rabelais was spreading his dream of an expansion of the human spirit in Europe, the call in Japan was "Ever smaller! Ever smaller!" This was personified by Mame-emon, the tiny hero of *Kontan iroasobi futokoro-otoko* (*The Amorous Intrigues of a Pocket-sized Man*) by Ejima Kiseki (1667–1736), and by the heroes of subsequent erotic stories of the Edo period (1603–1868). Ejima's story is part philosophy and part popular literature, and its fictitious hero clearly represented the aspirations of the common people. The ideal Ejima portrays through Mame-emon is not that of a giant like Gargantua but of a miniature man (*mame-otoko*) reduced to the size of a poppy seed.

Mame-emon, the hero of the story, is an ugly man who was conceived after his mother had dreamed she swallowed a horse. One day he meets a fairy from whom he receives some gold pills and a book of secret teachings. He is told that if he takes one of the pills he can shrink down to the size of a poppy seed, and if he enters a man's pocket in that form he can exchange souls with that man. He excitedly hurries off to Kyoto, where by virtue of the magic pills he gets involved in a variety of amorous adventures. Toward the end of the story he has entered the chamber of one of the ladies-in-waiting of a powerful lord and is mistaken for an insect. He is about to be crushed beneath a finger, but as luck would have it he is saved by the lord himself and is promoted into public service.

Like Issun Bōshi, Mame-emon is a little giant. The story of his adventures is a fine example of the paradoxical creed of "miniaturism": that "smaller is stronger." And the wide popularity of the book in the Edo period proves that its thesis was not held by its author alone. The book spawned numerous imitations; the name Mame-emon entered the popular vocabulary, and in its ordinary nominal form, *mame-otoko* (miniature man), it found its way into dictionaries. Miniature women, too, appeared in Edo period stories, among them *Junshoku eiga musume* (*Embellished Tales of a Woman of Splendor*), where the heroine's name is Omame (Little Bean).

Our thesis, then, is that one aspect of the Japanese mind is an imaginative power that seeks to make things smaller, that idealizes the dwarf over the giant. This has found expression in many forms of Japanese culture. It is seen in the miniature trees of *bonsai* and in rock gardens, where space itself is scaled down. In modern times, first the transistor and now the personal computer are evidence of this same tendency.

SMALLER IS BETTER: SIX EXAMPLES

Boxes within Boxes—The Principle of Inclusion

Tōkai no	On the white sand beach
kojima no iso no	Of a tiny island
shirasuna ni	In the Eastern Sea,
ware nakinurete	Bathed in tears,
kani to tawamuru	I toy with a crab.

This famous poem by Ishikawa Takuboku (1886–1912) literally reads like this: "On the white sand of a beach / Of a small island / Of the Eastern Sea, / I am damp from crying / And I toy with a crab." Within its thirty-one syllables, there is nothing in the way of vocabulary that would identify the poem as Japanese. Nor is there any particular feeling, no social or historical reference within it, that is peculiar to Japan. What is there then about this poem that makes it so Japanese? It is the poem's structure, or more specifically, its syntax. Consider for a moment the repetitious use of the possessive *no* (rendered as "of" in the literal English translation). In the lines *Tōkai no / kojima no iso no / shirasuna ni* (On the white sand of a beach / Of a small island / Of the Eastern Sea), the connective *no* is sandwiched into the phrase three times. Four nouns are connected in succession by the possessive particle *no*. Such a strange structure would never appear in Korean writing, either in prose or in poetry. Thus to translate the poem into Korean (or, for that matter, English), one must alter its syntax, and in so doing, the poem loses its appeal.

Korean and Japanese sentence structure are generally considered to be more or less the same. The major difference between the two languages is vocabulary, and it is normally argued that the special characteristics of each language are to be found in their lexical differences. In other words, just by changing the vocabulary (though not the word order) a Japanese sentence will become Korean; a Korean sentence, Japanese. This could not happen either between Japanese or Korean and Chinese or between one of the two and any of the Indo-European languages. But what is noteworthy about Takuboku's poem is the peculiarity of its syntax.

A joke that used to be popular among young Koreans who did not know much Japanese illustrates how odd Japanese syntax sometimes appears to Koreans: Why does a Japanese clock, however well made, always run several minutes behind a Korean clock? Because the Korean clock goes "tick-tock, tick-tock," while the Japanese clock goes "tick-tock *no* tick-tock *no.*"

This joke came about because often when Japanese tried to speak a few words of Korean they would pepper their Korean with a lot of unnecessary possessives. But it shows how even ordinary people noticed the fundamental syntactic difference between Japanese and Korean. This difference is so noticeable that even Korean children who do not know Takuboku's poem recognize that someone who uses a lot of possessives in his Korean speech is doing so in imitation of the Japanese language.

A number of examples illustrate the point. In Japanese, one does not say "starlight" but "star's light" (*hoshi no hikari*). Similarly, a Japanese would say "firefly's light" or "insect's chirp." A Korean, on the other hand, would omit the possessive and simply say "starlight," "firefly light," and "insect chirp." There can be very few other languages in the world—certainly Korean is not among them—that use possessives as much as Japanese. When Takuboku added not two but three possessives to his poem, he did so as a kind of toast to the Japanese language. And surely these possessives are the secret to the success of his poem.

What is the nature of that secret? It is the Japanese love for abbreviation, the tendency to reduce the complex to the simple in language. Why do the Japanese, inventors of the world's shortest poetic form, the *haiku*, use multiple possessives so frequently when most of the rest of us are trying to avoid them? Because, I believe, the possessive *no* functions as a vehicle for reducing in scale all manner of thoughts and forms. There is an intimate connection between the brevity of Takuboku's thirty-one syllable poem and his use of multiple possessives. The possessives are what allow Takuboku to achieve so much in so little space.

An analysis of the lines "On the white sand of a beach / Of a small island / Of the Eastern Sea" will make this clear. First, we must understand that the English syntax here is the exact opposite of the Japanese; an accurate but highly awkward English rendition of these lines would be: "On an Eastern Sea's / Small island's beach's / White sand." What Takuboku has done is to use the possessive *no* to reduce the vast, boundless "Eastern Sea" to a "small island." Then, with two more possessives he has further reduced the scene from "small island" to "beach" to "white sand." By the end of the poem, we are down to a tiny crab. And since the poet is weeping, we have in essence the great Eastern Sea in a single teardrop.

Takuboku's is not just an ordinary short poem. By means of the unique syntax of the Japanese language, he has shrunk the world, beginning with the Eastern Sea, down to the scale of a box garden. And this reduction is expressed in concrete linguistic form by the use of the three possessives. The essence of his poem does not lie in the surface meaning of the tears or the crab he describes. Rather, it is in his contracting of the scene of the Eastern Sea down to a crab and a teardrop, and in the structure he uses to that end. This manipulation of grammar allows him to produce a uniquely Japanese poem, one that could hardly have been created in any other language.

This feature can be found throughout Takuboku's poetry. Whatever the subject, his poems invariably exhibit this contracting structure, as for example in the following:

> *Haru no yuki*   Spring snow softly covers
> *Ginza no ura no*   Three stories of brick
> *sangai no*   On a backstreet in Ginza.
> *rengazukuri ni*
> *yawaraka ni furu*

> (Literal paraphrase: "Spring snow— / On Ginza's backstreet's / Three stories' / Brick building, / It softly falls.")

Although the scene is no longer the Eastern Sea but Ginza, in the middle of a big city, the characteristic use of possessives to reduce the scene in scale remains intact. Ginza is gradually scaled down to the roof of a three-story brick building just as the sea gave way to a tiny crab in the other poem. The movement is exactly the opposite of the ripples that occur when one tosses a stone into a pond. By the use of the possessive *no* the images of the poem form a series of successively contracting concentric rings. The force of the *no* is implosive rather than explosive.

By no means is this technique limited to Takuboku. Another fine instance of this can be found in the famous translation by Ueda Bin (1874–1916) of Verlaine's "Fallen Leaves." In one especially noteworthy line Ueda uses the word *no* four times (once in the nominative case, the other times as a possessive) where Verlaine uses *de* only twice. In so doing, the translator preserves the sonority of the original. To the Japanese ear, the much-maligned repetition of possessives becomes a kind of music.

The tradition of *no* is as old as Japanese literature itself. Take, for example, the following poem by Emperor Tenji (614–71):

Aki no ta no	Here in my flimsy hut
kariho no io no	Roughly thatched of cut grasses
toma o arami	Amid the autumn fields,
waga koromode wa	My robes are dampened
tsuyu ni nuretsutsu	By teardrops of dew.

(Literal paraphrase: "The roughness of the cut-grass thatching / Of my temporary hut / Of the fields of autumn— / My robes / Are wet with [tear]drops of dew.")

A story from the *Record of Ancient Matters*, Japan's oldest written history, also illustrates my point. Emperor Yūryaku, whose reign dates are traditionally given as 456–79, is having a banquet with some courtiers under a huge zelkova tree near the Hatsuse River. A leaf from the zelkova tree flutters down into the cup of saké a young lady-in-waiting has just served to the emperor. He strikes her for her laxity and is about to kill her when she recites an impromptu verse to the enormous tree, which seems to overarch the whole world. Preserving the use of possessives, it might roughly be rendered as follows: "A leaf of the tip of the branch of the top falls down to a branch of the middle; a leaf of the tip of the branch of the middle falls down to a branch of the bottom; a leaf of the tip of the branch of the bottom falls into the saké cup." Upon hearing this poem, it is said, the emperor pardoned the lady. In the poem, the heavens are reduced to a saké cup and the huge zelkova tree to a single leaf.

What is the cultural significance of our discussion? People have a particular outlook toward the world on the basis of which they interact with their environment. This outlook gives meaning and shape to the things with which it comes in contact. Culture manifests itself in various functional and qualitative forms, but in the long run all of these manifestations are produced by a common conscious outlook toward the world. This outlook, or orientation, shows itself in languages—in their structure more than their vocabulary. This is why I believe that the syntax formed by multiple use of the possessive *no* provides one clue toward understanding the unique structure of the Japanese consciousness. And once we have uncovered the secret of this *no*, we have arrived at the idiom of the Japanese consciousness, the essential Japanese outlook toward the world, and understood that this is to reduce the world in order to understand it, reduce the world in order to express it, reduce the world in order to manipulate it.

Takuboku did not see the elements of his poem—the Eastern Sea, the small island, the beach, the white sand—as a disordered jumble. He found a certain connection between the things that exist in space, and he brought to bear a specific viewpoint in organizing those elements into a poem. It would have been absolutely impossible for him, in the brevity of a thirty-one syllable poem, to have given explicit and particular descriptions of the world around him or of his own feelings. Instead, precisely because he fit them all into a consistent spatial framework, he was able to pull the elements together into a single unit. And this is why his poem is not long, indeed could not be long.

To Takuboku, the Eastern Sea in itself is too large. He can only understand it intimately if it envelops him. The only way he can "play with" the Eastern Sea is by conceiving of it in the form of a little crab that has a hold on his finger. This in turn produces the poem's ironic juxtaposition of alienation from and harmony with the world, expressed by the poet's weeping and playing at the same time. Without a reductive outlook toward the world Takuboku could not have written of such feelings.

The poetic device of reducing space by using a successive series of possessives is given concrete expression in the boxes-within-boxes so popular with the Japanese, each box slightly smaller and fitting inside a larger box. Not only boxes. We also find pans-within-pans and bowls-within-bowls (the latter usually coming in sets of seven). The boxes-within-boxes principle allows a large number of objects to be stored in a small space and makes them easier to carry around.

Since ancient times the Japanese have favored this convenient, compact, and functional way of making sets of utensils. A three-meter pole made in this manner can be telescoped into a pole half a meter long. A boat constructed in this way can be dismantled and the pieces fitted together so that it makes a box that can be carried about on land. In fact, during the Edo period (1603–1868) the Japanese used just such poles-within-poles and "folding boats."

The reductive structure of successive possessives finds verbal expression in brief and beautiful poems. It finds concrete expression in the portable and convenient utensils made like boxes-within-boxes. These two manifestations are splendidly united in this *haiku* by one of the poets of the Mino school:

> *Suzushisa ya*   Cool lakes nestle
> *umi o ireko no*   Among mountains within mountains,
> *Hakone yama*   The Hakone range.

The Fan—Fold It, Hold It, Bring It Closer

The simplest, clearest example of the Japanese propensity for making things smaller is the folding fan (*ōgi*, or *sensu*). The Chinese character used to write the word "fan" originally meant "door panel," indicating its broad, flat shape. Almost every society in the world has its version of a flat, open fan, called *uchiwa* in Japanese. We can imagine the earliest humans fanning themselves with leaves of trees whenever they needed a cooling breeze.

In the *Gu jin zhu*, a Chinese encyclopedia compiled about A.D. 300, it is claimed that the flat fan was invented by the legendary Emperor Shun in the second millennium B.C. It describes this first fan as being made from the tail feathers of a quail. In Egypt a superb flat fan dated the fourteenth century B.C. was unearthed from Tutankhamen's tomb. Yet both the Chinese and Egyptian fans are rigid, flat, and of fixed shape.

Gradually the materials used to make rigid fans became more sophisticated, evolving from leaves to feathers and then paper. Rigid fans made of paper already existed as art objects by the fourth century A.D. in China. And the Korean history *Samguk sagi* (*History of the Three Kingdoms*) relates that even before the Koryŏ dynasty beautiful fans made to look like peacock feathers were exchanged as gifts of the highest value. It seems likely that the rigid fan made its way into Japan from China and Korea. But as soon as the fan arrived in Japan it underwent a revolutionary metamorphosis, and the folding fan was born.

Legend has it that the folding fan was invented by the Empress Jingū (traditional reign dates, A.D. 201–69) during the Japanese conquest of Korea. She is supposed to have been inspired when she saw the wings of a bat. Whatever the truth of this explanation, it does seem that it was in Japan the folding fan was first used.

Delving into the historical records of the folding fan, one finds that it represents an unusual countervailing current in the normal flow of culture. The *Song shi* (*History of the Song Dynasty*, compiled in 1345) relates that the Japanese priest Kiin brought folding fans with him as gifts when he visited the Song court. It notes that he presented, among other things, "one lacquer fan box decorated with gold and silver dust, twelve cypress folding fans and two 'bat wing' fans." In another Song dynasty chronicle the writer tells of his surprise at seeing a Japanese folding fan being sold by a merchant, and he describes the fan in detail. One Ming dynasty record states flatly that "there were no such things as folding fans in ancient China," and another indicates that the folding fan was first introduced into China by barbarians from the southeast. At least one Korean record also indicates that China did not originally have the folding fan, and that the Chinese used rigid fans similar to the ones used in Korea.

Neither the Egyptians who built the pyramids nor the Greeks who constructed the Parthenon ever felt the breeze of a folding fan. Originally there were no folding fans anywhere in Europe. They did not arrive until Portuguese merchants opened trade routes to China in the fifteenth century. Even then, it was not until the seventeenth century that the use of folding fans became widespread. French Impressionists such as Degas and Manet would gather at a Paris cabaret where the waitresses wore kimono and folding fans hung on the walls.

There existed, however, something known as the "Koryŏ fan." According to Chinese records from the Sung and Ming dynasties, China first got folding fans of pine wood from the kingdom of Koryŏ in Korea. Japanese scholars assert that the Chinese probably mistook as Korean fans what were really Japanese in origin. They theorize that the Japanese folding fans found their way to Korea and from there to China. This is not the place to enter into the controversy. Suffice it to say that since the human figures painted on the so-called Koryŏ fans are wearing Japanese-style clothing, the theory that folding fans originated in Japan would seem to carry more weight. In any case, regardless of who first invented the folding fan, the fact remains that it is the Japanese who are most fond of it. We are told that when the Chinese first saw a collapsible fan in the Song dynasty they greeted it with "derisive smiles." A long time passed before it was widely accepted by the Chinese people; for a great while it was only used by courtesans. To the eyes of those on the Asian mainland, the small folding fan must have looked like a toy. The expansive Chinese could not understand the Japanese propensity for reducing things in size.

How did the Japanese come to invent the folding fan? Scholars have proposed several hypotheses.

One scholar has suggested that rigid fans of paper covering a frame were introduced from China. The Japanese already had a similar type of fan using *birō* palm leaves instead of paper (even now in Kyushu fans are made this way) and the *birō* palm leaf, when grasped at the sides, tends to fold up like an accordion. Someone, this scholar argues, had the idea of joining the properties of the Chinese paper fan and the palm leaf. By tying strips of cypress wood together so that they could be opened and closed, the cypress fan was invented. Another scholar has theorized that the idea of the folding fan came from the *shaku*, a kind of ceremonial baton, since the ribs of the earliest cypress folding fans are similar in shape to the cypress *shaku*, and since both the cypress folding fan and the *shaku* were ceremonial articles in the imperial court. Still another theory has it that the idea came from ancient wooden clappers that were made by gathering several wood strips together, drilling a hole in each of them, and tying them together with a cord.

Of course, it was not really an external stimulus such as a palm leaf, a ceremonial baton, or a set of wooden clappers that brought about the folding fan. Rather, it was born of the Japanese propensity toward making things—in this case, the rigid fan— smaller. In the folding fan, we see a metaphor for Japanese culture itself.

In one sense, a folding fan is just a shrunken rigid fan. It simply takes the form and materials of the rigid fan and folds them so that they can be easily held in the hand. In geometric terms, it is a plane become a line. The effect of this is that the rigid fan, which can only exist apart from the user, becomes something that can be easily drawn in and held close to one's body. As the tenth-century priest-poet Ekei wrote:

> Half hidden in the sleeve,
> A folding fan;
> It calls to mind the moon
> Not yet emerged.

The folding fan is a rigid fan one can store in one's sleeve. If a rigid fan is the moon, a folding fan is the moon in its potential state, "not yet emerged."

A *haiku* by Shigetsugu puts the matter even more clearly:

The sun, the moon
Both held in one hand—
A Shura fan.

The Shura fan, favored by warriors and also used on the Nō stage, was made with a black frame and usually bore a painting of the sun and the moon. Ekei's moon "half hidden in the sleeve" becomes in Shigetsugu's poem a moon "held in the hand." On the surface, of course, Shigetsugu is referring to a sun and a moon painted on the fan, but on a more abstract level his fan is a means by which the larger world, the distant celestial world, can be brought close to us and reduced to fit into a human hand. To fold up a fan is to shrink the world itself. Rather than objectifying space by leaving it as a wide, flat plane, folding a fan is a concrete way to make that infinite plane, the world, easier to grasp. Thus, in the way the Japanese went about reducing the fan we can learn a great deal about Japanese epistemology, aesthetics, and practicality.

We must understand that the folding fan's primary importance was as a tool for understanding the world; it was not just a practical utensil for directing a cooling breeze toward oneself. Originally it was treated as a ceremonial object for use in court rituals. It was not until the seventeenth century that it began to be used by common people as a practical cooling device. Looked at in this historical light, it is clear that what lay behind the shrinking of the rigid fan into a folding fan was more than mere practicality. The folding fan was seen as a way to understand reality and as a symbol of reality itself.

Not only have the folding fans made specifically for use in religious ceremonies always been treated as ritual objects; so too have the ordinary cypress or paper folding fans. From ancient times, they have customarily been bestowed as gifts of appreciation on dutiful retainers. Folding fans were not only used for cooling oneself, they have also always been an indispensible accessory in a formal clothing ensemble. The reason why folding fans, unlike rigid fans, have taken on ritual meaning and have long been given as tokens of esteem is because of their significance as symbols of the Japanese perception of reality.

Because a folding fan can be closed, it can also be opened. The folding and unfolding of a fan is a way of grasping the mysteries of reality, for the opening and closing of a fan is like the folding and unfolding of fate, and the movement involved in creating and diverting a breeze with a fan is, literally and figuratively, a kind of beckoning. It is a way of having a direct experience of the world by giving concrete form to a vague, formless reality and of bringing that form close to oneself.

One of the purposes of religious ceremony is to give concrete form to the transcendent, thereby making it more understandable. Special folding fans perform the same function and thus are used in such rituals as the tea ceremony and funerals, and in earlier times monks used them like prayer beads.

Therefore, in the reduction of the flat fan to a folding fan we can also see the concepts of beckoning, drawing closer, and holding. In the Japanese mind the tendency is not to face out toward the world and the transcendent gods and move toward them, it is to beckon them inward and draw them closer to oneself. In most ages in most other countries the wind in literature is associated with images of something being blown away. But in Japan the wind is something which *comes to* you from the other world, something which envelops you. In other words, the image is of beckoning, or drawing closer. One scholar has counted more than forty poems in the great thirteenth-century poetry anthology *Shinkokin-shū* that use the phrase "the wind comes blowing" (*kaze zo fuku*) in this manner.

In Japanese mythology there is a story of a artful person who called the sun back up by waving a fan. This upsetting of the natural order incurred the wrath of the gods and brought about the fan wielder's downfall. In *haiku*, there are countless poems about drawing the moon closer. Koreans have written many poems in praise of the moon. But these poets did not beckon the moon to draw it closer. They sought to leave this world and rise to the moon's level of reality. This attitude is found in an old Korean folk song that can be paraphrased as follows: "With a gold and silver ax, I shall cut down the moon's laurel tree and with it make a three-room hut, there to live forever with my mother and father."

But Japanese *haiku* poets beckon the moon from its distant setting and try to draw it closer, like a folded fan. Take, for instance, the moon of Ryōkan, poet and Zen priest (1758–1831):

> A thief—
> At least he left behind
> The moon at my window.

Or Issa's moon:

> Hey, you kids!
> Which one of yours is it,
> This red moon?

The contracting quality of the fan also gives it a pivotal role in Japanese aesthetics, for a fan can be folded up and the painting carried along in one's pocket. The folding fan is portable art. By analogy, we can easily see why Japanese prefer picture scrolls, which can readily be rolled up and carried, to the immovable picture in a frame. In order to paint a picture on the small surface of a folding fan one has to reduce the size of the subject, be it a flower or a mountain, to tiny dimensions. Then, as one folds up the fan, the subject gets even tinier.

The crafting of the folding fan is in itself an exercise in reduction. To make a cypress fan one must shave thick boards into paper-thin slices. The technique displays an aesthetic consciousness oriented toward the small and finely detailed.

The folding fan is also an integral part of the performing arts, indispensible to traditional Japanese dance and the dance performed in Nō plays. Indeed, Nō actors insist that the fan actually creates the art of a Nō dance. Of the fan in Nō drama, Paul Claudel wrote: "It is a flower in glorious bloom, a blazing torch in the hand, a moment of quiet contemplation, the resounding of demons." Kabuki, too, requires a fan. In short, where there is a fan, there is painting, there is dance, there is drama.

The very shape of the folding fan—a semicircle that demonstrates perfectly the concept of contraction—is considered by Japanese to be a model of beauty. By coincidence, it is also the shape of Mount Fuji.

No matter how wide one opens a folding fan, it is still limited by its basic shape, which was designed with contraction in mind. Its semicircular form is straining with potential for contraction. When the fan is open, this strain is most intense at the pivot, so the tendency of the fan is toward closing rather than opening. The folding fan shows the opposite of the Western concept of perspective: it gets larger and wider as one moves toward the edge—a kind of reverse perspective. Japanese paintings and gardens often show this kind of reverse perspective, and perhaps the folding fan gave birth to the concept.

This said, we must not forget the folding fan's practical function. Toward the end of the Heian period, in the twelfth century, folding fans were being mass-produced in Kyoto. Although solid evidence is hard to find, Hata Koretatsu, in his book *Yomo no suzuri* (*The Four-sided Inkstone*), states: "The present-day custom of attaching the suffix *ya* [literally, 'house'] to a shop's name originated with fan shops, which always used that suffix in their names." If this is true, then the making and selling of fans must have represented one of Japan's earliest ventures into commercialism.

Japan's fan commerce was not limited to the domestic market. From the earliest times of production in Kyoto, Japanese paper fans were being sold in China. This fan trade lasted until the Muromachi period (1336–1568), and during that time China imported Japanese fans and then reexported them to Europe. Thus the honor of being the first Japanese good to dominate the world market would appear to belong to the folding fan.

Why did the Japanese folding fan become an international commodity? Probably because it was more compact, thus more portable and convenient, than the rigid fan, and because of its novelty. To make a product smaller and more convenient and to make an unusual product that nonetheless elicits the response, "Why didn't anyone think of this before?"—these have always been the qualities of Japanese goods, in the past as today.

Just as the concept of inclusiveness created the "boxes-within-boxes culture," so the concept of folding-up made possible a number of characteristically Japanese objects, the folding fan preeminent among them. The Japanese sought to fold up everything they saw. They even tried to fold up the walls that separate rooms, and the result was the *fusuma*, a sliding paper-covered door on a wooden frame that surely must be the world's most flexible "wall." The Japanese paper lantern closely resembles Chinese and Korean models, with one important difference: the Japanese version folds up. Because of their flexibility, even the largest of lanterns can, like the fan, be folded up flat for storage.

The Japanese proclivity to fold things up shows no signs of waning. During the Taishō era (1912–26) sliding umbrellas were introduced from Germany. By 1950 the Japanese had made the first collapsible umbrella. Just as happened with the fan in the past, the Japanese took something and made it smaller, then turned around and reexported it, gaining control of the market in the process. In the early 1980s, the Japanese developed an even smaller umbrella, one that folds three ways and is the world's shortest, measuring eighteen centimeters. Now the umbrella, just like the fan, can fit in your pocket.

Then there is the transistor, which after the war helped Japan break into the international marketplace. This, too, was made possible by the Japanese belief that in order to make something more manageable, more compact, and more functional, one has to make it smaller. In a sense, then, the "transistor culture" goes all the way back to the Heian period. Japanese folding fans, nothing more than imported Chinese rigid fans reduced in size then reexported, produced a miracle by taking the functionalist West by storm, a storm that today shows no signs of abating. It has its latest manifestation in smaller, simpler cameras and electrical household appliances, not to mention the more sophisticated world of VSLIs.

Although the Japanese imported the basic idea for many of these products from China or the West, their special contribution was in reducing them to fit the hand, and this allowed Japanese products to take the lead.

In the case of fans, eventually the Chinese market became flooded, and they were no longer considered desirable items. Some Japanese scholars suggest that as a consequence Japanese merchants turned to threats and eventually force to market their goods, and this was the origin of the notorious *wakō*, the Japanese pirates of the fifteenth century—an early example, perhaps, of trade friction. Historical sources indicate that by the fifteenth century the Chinese, for their part, associated the fan trade with Japanese piracy and loathed both. How little things have changed!

The Anesama Doll—Take Away And Pare Down

The concept of reduction is most clearly seen in miniatures. To miniaturize something is to take an actual object and shrink it in size with all the details intact so that it becomes an exact but smaller copy of the original. The Japanese yield to no other people in their ability to do this, as we can tell from a glance at the records of "the world's smallest." The world's tiniest miniature airplane is 1.6 millimeters long and has a wingspan of 1 millimeter, making it smaller than a common housefly. This little plane won the grand prize at the 1970 World Paper Airplane Convention in the United States. It was made in Japan, the work of Takewaka Hiroshi of Shiga Prefecture. Japan also takes the laurel wreath for the world's smallest motorcycle. It is 17.5 centimeters long and weighs 1.7 kilograms. Its tires, casters borrowed from a chair, are five centimeters in diameter. The engine, of the type used in model airplanes, is started by a battery. Its inventor, Hasegawa Shūji of Tokyo, is said to have ridden 10 meters on it.

To succeed in miniaturizing, delicacy and subtlety are required. Japanese have long competed in writing characters on grains of rice. Yoshida Godō is a gold medalist in three events of the "Miniwriting Olympics," having written 600 characters on a grain of rice, 160 characters on a sesame seed, and 3,000 characters on a soybean. From writing we move to etching, and the record here is forty-six characters carved into a grain of rice, and carved in the scarcely credible time of about a minute. It is not surprising to find that Japan has a Museum of Micro Art, where some 20,000 examples of miniature writing, all of which require a magnifying glass to be seen, are stored.

Dolls provide the best of yardsticks for measuring the extent of the Japanese penchant for the miniature. Every society, at least at its primitive stage, has used dolls as magic tokens to word off evil spirits or ensure prosperity. It is hard to imagine a primitive society without dolls. But when it comes to finding a true "doll culture," a country where dolls are more than just magical objects, where they are appreciated as toys and as objects of beauty, Japan stands preeminent, at least among the countries of East Asia. This is one of the most notable ways in which Japanese culture differs from that of China and Korea.

Although both these countries share many religious rituals with Japan, neither has anything like the Japanese doll festival, *hina matsuri*. If anything, in Korea there has traditionally been something of a taboo against dolls, and until modern times it was unthinkable that children should play with them. Yet dolls have been enjoyed in Japan at least since the Heian period (794–1184). In *The Tale of Genji* we find Murasaki's nurse admonishing her: "This year you must try to act a little more grown up. They say that people should no longer play with dolls past the age of ten."

Sei Shōnagon, too, discusses the subject of dolls in her *Pillow Book*, which often reads like a testament to the Japanese love for things tiny and nowhere more so than in the following passage:

> Beautiful [*utsukushi*] things:
> The face of a child drawn on a melon.
> A baby sparrow that comes hopping over when someone imitates a mouse's squeak. . . .
> It is most adorable [*utsukushi*] when a one- or two-year-old baby who is crawling around quickly spots with his sharp eyes a tiny bit of something and picks it up in his charming little fingers to show it to some adult. . . .
> The objects used in the Doll Festival.
> A tiny floating lotus leaf picked from a pond; a small hollyhock flower; indeed, all things small, no matter what they are, all things small are beautiful.

In the very word *utsukushii* (modern meaning, "beautiful"; classical meaning, "adorable, beautiful") we can see the tendency toward miniaturization found in the "doll culture." The Chinese character used to write *utsukushii* (Chinese, "*mei*") is made up of the component "sheep" over the component "large," and in Chinese it originally denoted something large and bounteous, like a well-fed sheep. The original meaning of the Korean word that uses the same character is not known for certain, but it apparently indicated something full and complete. The Japanese word *utsukushii*, however, as shown by the above passage from *The Pillow Book*, indicates an affection for what is small and pretty. The meaning seems to have evolved from the sense of "cute" or "adorable."

Seen in this light it becomes clear why Japan alone among the countries of East Asia is the land of dolls.

It is not simply a matter of doll appreciation having a long history in Japan. The fact is, there are nearly as many types of dolls in Japan as there are stars in the sky: unclothed dolls, dolls wearing kimono, dolls in complementary sets, dolls carved of wood then painted, male and female dolls made of paper or brocade, tiny dolls used in miniature scenes—the list goes on and on. In terms of variety of material and designs, there is no nation East or West that can match Japan. As the names of the various types of doll indicate (for example, *hina* (chick) dolls and "poppy seed dolls"), Japanese dolls are nearly always small and delicate.

Among the types of Japanese doll, perhaps the best example of the Japanese approach to miniaturization is the *anesama ningyō*, the "big sister doll." These dolls are not perfect miniature copies of some larger object. Whether they be made of paper or straw, and no matter what regional variations they exhibit, all *anesama* dolls have one common defining characteristic: they have no arms or legs. They demonstrate the simplification aspect of the Japanese tendency to make things smaller. Pare down the extremities of the human figure and you arrive at a shape exactly like that of the *anesama* doll: a round head and body that is a smooth line. Thus the charm of the *anesama* doll arises from the basic simplicity of its shape rather than from its being a detailed miniaturization of a larger model.

This armless, legless reduction of the human form can also be seen in the *kokeshi* doll, which is essentially a wooden dowel with a round ball attached to the end, the whole assembly being painted to represent a human. *Kokeshi* dolls are made and sold in and around the hot springs of northeastern Honshu, and their history is not so very old. They apparently came about independently of the *anesama* doll, one explanation being that they were made by carpenters who carved wooden bowls for a living. Although the origin of the name *kokeshi* is obscure, it is thought to be a corruption of a phrase meaning "people of whittled-down wood." If that is the case, we can say that both the *anesama* doll and the *kokeshi* doll sprang from the same approach to reduction: take away and whittle down. And this tells us much about that aspect of the Japanese character that seeks beauty and function by simplifying things.

By the same token, we can surmise that there is more than just the influence of Zen Buddhism to the Japanese love of Daruma, the legendary founder of Zen, who is usually depicted as having no arms or legs. It is traditionally said that Daruma meditated in a sitting posture for nine straight years facing a wall, thus causing his extremities to wither away and fall off. But Daruma's shape as commonly represented in Japan is similar enough to that of *anesama* and *kokeshi* dolls to suggest a different explanation for his popularity.

Boldly cutting away that which is wasteful or too complicated—the armless, legless form of the *anesama* doll has found its way into all aspects of Japanese aesthetics. It can be seen in the Japanese flag, surely the simplest design among all the flags of the world, and in the Shinto shrine gate, made of nothing but two supports and a crossbar.

This tendency to simplify, to take something and pare it down, can also be detected in Japanese literature and language. Both Korea and Japan used Chinese characters before they developed writing systems of their own. But there is a big difference in the way the two countries went about making writing systems for themselves. The Korean alphabet, called Hangul, is abstract and phonetic, based solely on sound, and bears no relation to Chinese characters. In simple terms, in the Korean phonetic alphabet, letters were invented to suit each particular morpheme. But the Japanese phonetic syllabary, called *kana*, uses simplified shapes based on Chinese characters. We might say that the Japanese phonetic letters are like the *anesama* doll in that they are Chinese characters whose arms and legs have been whittled down. The resulting letters are free of complexity.

Like the doll without arms and legs, Japanese words and phrases are often abbreviated into a "head." This results in a degree of linguistic truncation rarely found in other languages. It is exemplified by the much-used expression *dōmo*, the basic meaning of which is "very [much]," "quite," "somehow." Since *dōmo* is an adverb it functions at most as a kind of hat or gloves covering the word modified. Its role presupposes that there is a verbal "head" or "hands" to be covered, but the Japanese often cut away the word modified, leaving just the adverb *dōmo*. *Dōmo*, translated here as "how very," appears in a great many different expressions, such as: "how very grateful I am," "how very sad," "how very fortunate," and "how very rude of me." These are usually shortened to the single word *dōmo*, "how very," and yet the Japanese understand each other perfectly well. Indeed, to the Japanese it seems quite natural. It is a product of the reduction mentality. Similar things have happened to expressions of greeting in Japanese, such as *konnichiwa* (literally, "today is—"), *konbanwa* (literally, "this evening is—"), and *tada ima* (literally, "just now—"). *Konnichiwa* is short for "*today is* a fine day, isn't it?" *Konbanwa* is short for "*this evening* is a fine evening, isn't it?" *Tada ima* is short for "*just now* I have returned safely." The main body of the sentence has been cut off, leaving only the little cap at the head, just as with expressions using *dōmo*.

Nor is this eagerness to abbreviate something new. The historian Inagaki Motoi relates a story in his book *Nihon no shiro*

(*Japanese Castles*) that illustrates how this odd linguistic tradition affected speech in the Edo period:

> One peaceful day at the castle, a young page's voice was heard calling out the strange syllable "*mō*." From the lord's inner rooms in the main part of the castle, "*mō, mō!*" echoed through the castle grounds. It was not some bovine alarm clock, but the page boy's own unique abbreviation for "*Mō, omezame de gozaru*" ("It is *already* time for his Lordship to wake up").

In the same way, foreign words are incorporated into the Japanese language, then abbreviated. For example, *torēshingu peipa* (tracing paper) becomes *torepe*, *tēpu rekōda* (tape recorder) becomes *tereko*, and *mazā konpurekkusu* (mother complex) becomes *mazakon*. The expression *imeiji chienji* (image change) is abbreviated to *imechie*. The older generation in Japan probably remembers with fondness the phrase *moga mobo*, short for "modern girl, modern boy." There is no end to the number of terms like this.

Besides demonstrating one aspect of the reduction principle—that of "take away and pare down"—the *anesama* doll also embodies another: that of concentration on one point and intensification. Although the doll has no arms or legs, almost obsessive attention is paid to the details of the hair, which becomes the main feature of the doll. So much that is miniaturized in Japan has one point on which attention has been concentrated. On the one hand there is abbreviation, on the other, emphasis.

The hairstyles of *anesama* dolls are a complicated affair, and there are scores of types. They are arranged in order from forelocks, to sidelocks, to bun on top of the head, and there are numerous ways in which to make these arrangements. The overall image a particular doll presents is determined by the details of its hairstyle. For example, if the topknot known as the Shimada style is pulled upward, the doll appears younger; if it is pulled slightly downward, the effect is thought to be chic. To form these styles, the hair is tied with raw silk thread or paper cords, and each style has its appropriate ornaments. The hair ornaments themselves are a showcase of the miniature. For example, an elaborate ornamental hairpin overflows with yellow, red, and pink artificial flowers so tiny they would be hard to hold even with a pair of tweezers. All of the various ornaments are like tiny, detailed inhabitants of a dreamlike microcosm of the world.

There is even a third aspect of the reduction principle to be found in the *anesama* doll: that of implicitly changing front to back. The *anesama* doll is decorated to show off the back. Japanese women also dress this way when wearing the traditional kimono, which is adorned so that the rear view is the important one. This custom is surely particular to Japan; only in Japan is the back emphasized. This is done through the hairstyle, the collar pulled back so that the nape of the neck is clearly visible, and the decorative tying of the sash. The front, the face, conveys a clear message. But the rear view of the formal hairstyle, tied up and held together with ornaments, conveys silence and hesitation. It is cryptic, and leads one into darkness. But by decorating the *anesama* doll to "show off the back," the Japanese bring speech to a silent world, movement to a still world, and light to darkness.

The Well-Stuffed Box Lunch—Pack It In

Now what, you may ask, is so special about box lunches? This, for a start: There are, according to a survey taken in 1978, more than eighteen hundred types of box lunches sold at railway stations alone. Seven hundred of these types are some ordinary variation or other of the "big three" of box lunch ingredients: scrambled eggs rolls, fish paste, and fish. The other eleven hundred feature some special delicacy, and such box lunches have gained in number in recent years.

Some travel guides now give descriptions and maps of all the railway-station box lunches to be found throughout the Japanese archipelago. But to really learn about the box lunch, you must go to Kyoto, the Mecca of Japanese cooking. There you will find the "moon series" of box lunches: the New Moon Box Lunch, the Round Moon Box Lunch, and the Half Moon Box Lunch. You will find box lunches named after famous masters of the tea ceremony and aesthetes such as Sen no Rikyū and Hon'ami Kō-etsu. You will also find a "great lunch-box lunch series" featuring box lunches in bamboo boxes, or tea boxes, or little pails, or willow boxes.

When people hear the word "box lunch," most of them probably think of blue-collar workers and the box lunches their wives prepare for them. But the concept of the box lunch goes all the way back to the Momoyama period (1568–1603), and it is yet another example of the Japanese tendency to make things smaller. For the box lunch is nothing more than the contents of a food tray, off which the Japanese still eat when in formal surroundings, reduced to fit into a box.

There are many explanations regarding the origin of the box lunch and the etymology of the Japanese word for box lunch, *bentō*. Some believe the box lunch originated with the uniform provisions the general Oda Nobunaga (1534–82) gave his troops. Others say it began in the early eighteenth century as a snack eaten between acts at the theater. Whatever the true origins, it is at least certain that the box lunch developed to fulfill the need for food that could be packed in a compact, handy container and carried around.

I suggest we need to take a closer look at why and how the box lunch evolved as a reduced and portable version of the food served on a tray. The *Ryūteiki*, an eighteenth-century book of essays, states that the word *bentō* is an abbreviated form of a phrase meaning roughly "just right (*tō*) for use as provisions (*ben*)," and was used to describe food reduced to fit into a box. But there is another Japanese word for box lunch which is totally self-explanatory: *kōchū*, "traveling kitchen."

The reason a "box lunch culture" evolved in Japan is because Japanese food lends itself to being clumped together and tightly packed. Korea remained a stranger to box lunches because, although rice is a staple there too, food is served in a different form.

Just compare Japanese and Korean pickles. Japanese pickles are not prepared or served in a broth, as they are in Korea. They appear in a clump. And compare Japanese and Korean soups. Japanese soup, as its name, *tsuyu*, implies, is mainly liquid, with just a bit of gluten or *tōfu* (bean curd) floating in it. But in Korean seaweed or beansprout soup, there are much larger quantities of those solid ingredients. Japanese food can be easily divided into solid and liquid types, but in Korea soup contains much solid matter, and solid food is usually served in a soup. Koreans do not like things without a broth; rather than clearly distinguishing the types of food served, they prefer to blur those distinctions. In fact, one of the worst insults in the Korean language is to say that someone or something is "without broth." Consequently, when eating a meal, Japanese use only chopsticks, whereas Koreans use both chopsticks and a spoon in equal measure.

How then is the reduction tendency characterized in the box lunch? Since a box lunch is the meal from a large, spacious food tray reduced so that it fits in a box, reduction, in this context, is synonymous with "packing in." "Packing in," indeed, is one important aspect of the reduction tendency.

This run-of-the-mill phrase, "packing in," is not limited to food. Just as when the Japanese see something, they feel tempted to fold it up, like the folding fan, or to place it inside something else, like the boxes-within-boxes, or to remove its extremities and simplify it, like the *anesama* doll, so when they see things scattered about, they wish to gather them up and put them in a box. The idea of gathering together can also be expressed as a "packing together" (the suggestion is of a lot of people gathered in a small place). "Packed in" can also mean to be stuck in a place, and the place itself can be called a "packed-in place," *tsumesho*, a word generally used to mean guardhouse, station, or office. Even the big final scene of a play or novel is referred to in Japanese as a "great packing in," *ōzume*.

There is no word in Korean that exactly describes the Japanese concept of "packing in." The closest we can come is the word *ch'aeyuda*, which means "fill up," but it does not imply the tension of things packed perfectly into a fixed frame. Thus canned goods, which in Japanese are called *kanzume* (literally, "packed in a can"), are called in Korean *t'ongjorim* (literally, "can cooked").

The concept of "packing in" applies not only to things; it has a psychological dimension too. A man who knows where he is going, who is firm of purpose and action, is "firmly pulled together" (*shikkari shite iru*), which means essentially that his attention, his spirit, is packed in tightly in readiness. Similarly, if you wish to apply your efforts seriously, earnestly, and diligently to something, you have to "pack in." It is not enough just to see, think, or breathe. In order to apply yourself to these activities with sufficient vigor, you have to "pack yourself into" them. Try, for example, "packing yourself into seeing" (*mitsumeru*, to stare hard at something), "packing yourself into thinking" (*omoitsumeru*, to take something to heart, to brood), or "packing in your breathing" (*iki o tsumeru*, to remain breathless and still).

Japanese skills manifest themselves in tightly packed situations. To the Japanese, therefore, something that cannot be packed in is worthless, *tsumaranai*, which literally means "not packed in." Once upon a time, people who did not fit snugly into the framework of a village were ostracized, treated as worthless. Nowadays, company staff training courses are an exercise in packing in knowledge and pulling the spirit together.

Democracy arose as a philosophy rooted in the concept of the multiplicity of individuals. But in Japan, individuals gain power only after they have been packed into a particular framework. (This is the cohesiveness for which the Japanese are so well known.) Japan, which is often referred to as the only liberal democracy in East Asia, is really a kind of totalitarian state that forces all of its population to fit into a small framework, just as food is reduced and packed into a lunch box.

"Packing in" is not limited to putting together things of a like nature. If anything, the exercise is enhanced when diversity and size are involved. Take, for instance, the screen painting by Kanō Eitoku (1543–90) known as *Scenes in and around Kyoto*. Into this one screen painting Eitoku packed all the life of every district of Kyoto and showed each of the four seasons as well. Not only are we shown all the incidental details, but people of every social class and every occupation, and even Portuguese and other foreigners, too. We see the same phenomenon in Buddhism, whose vast, abstract thought is reduced and packed into the two short incantations—*Namu Amida Butsu* (Hail to the Amida Buddha) and *Namu Myōhō Rengekyō* (Hail to the Magnificent Lotus Sutra)—of the two most popular streams of Japanese Buddhism. The chanting of these phrases is in itself sufficient to gain salvation.

We discussed earlier how by shaving off the extremities of Chinese characters, much in the manner that the *anesama* doll's arms and legs are cut off, the Japanese created "letters" for their phonetic alphabet. This demonstrated the principle of "paring down" or "taking away." But what happens when the box lunch principle, the principle of packing in, is applied to Chinese characters? The Japanese then come up with characters of their own, which we might call Japanese ideographs, which do not appear even in the most authoritative of Chinese dictionaries.

Let's look at some examples. Since a younger brother stands in his elder brother's shadow, the character element for "man" and that for "younger brother" were combined to make a Japanese ideograph meaning "shadow," as in "a shadow of his former self."

The Japanese work ethic is graphically reflected in the Japanese ideograph for "work," which is made up of the elements "man" and "move." Similarly, the elements for "stop" and "wind" are fitted nicely together to form the Japanese ideograph for "lull." None of these characters exists in Chinese or in Korean.

In the world of books, the "packing in" aspect of the reduction tendency is seen in pocket-sized paperbacks. Of course, Japan is not the only country with such books, but whereas the popularity of paperback books in the West is a postwar phenomenon, the Iwanami publishing house has been putting out its pocket-sized Akagi Series since before 1927. A passage in *Fūsetsu ni taete: Iwanami bunkō no hanashi* (*Weathering the Blizzard: the Story of the Iwanami Pocket Library*) describes the early Akagi editions: "These ten-cent books were about the same size as our later pocket-sized books; it did not matter how large the original book was, it was always reduced to just one tiny volume." The first true pocket library editions appeared in Japan in 1927. In its issue of 10 July 1927, the *Asahi* newspaper announced in a banner headline on the front page: "Books Ancient and Modern, East and West." Next to this was a manifesto stating, "We wish to make truth available to all the people" and an advertisement for Iwanami's Pocket Library.

On Japanese bookshelves, alongside the pocket libraries stand the concise dictionaries. Although small enough to fit easily into the hand, they have a total word count similar to that of a full-sized dictionary. Surely these are the dictionaries of Japan's reduction culture. I remember clearly when I first picked up a concise dictionary. I was in junior high school and had just started studying English. At the time, what was more important to me than the convenience of that dictionary for looking up words was the feeling of symbolic security I had from being able to hold a large number of English words in one hand.

Nevertheless, despite the concise dictionaries and despite the inundation of foreign words in the Japanese language, the

Japanese are not the world's greatest linguists, and one wonders if it might not be the fault of that wonderful "concise culture" represented by those little dictionaries. Learning a foreign language is a lot like sailing into uncharted seas. It requires an expansive way of thinking. And this is something the Japanese lack. They shun what is expansive and prefer what is small and can fit in the hand. The result is that they end up learning "concise" English, and stop there.

"The great books, ancient and modern, East and West" reduced to a pocket library; a palm-sized dictionary containing ten thousand entries—since this is what makes Japanese people feel that culture is intimately accessible, the pocket library and the concise dictionary are two elements that contribute to the development of the Japanese consciousness.

The Nō Mask—Assuming a Proper Attitude

Hokusai's *The Wave*, part of a series of woodblock prints called *Thirty-six Views of Mount Fuji*, is a superb representation of nature, of a tremendous wave. It leaves the viewer breathless, wide-eyed with wonder, and perhaps even speechless. Such was the opinion of the art critic Herbert Read as expressed in his book *The Meaning of Art* (London: Faber, 1931). He continued:

> Our feelings are absorbed by the sweep of the enormous wave, we enter into its upwelling movement, we feel the tension between its heave and the force of gravity, and as the crest breaks into foam, we feel that we ourselves are stretching angry claws against the alien objects beneath us.

But why does this feeling arise in us when we look at that wave? Perhaps it is the boldness of the composition, with the wave shown from so close up. Could it be the way lines are used to convey a sense of the wave's volume? Or could it be the contrast between the immobile Mount Fuji off in the distance and the prow of the boat about to be swallowed up by the wave? No, I think it is something different. I think the feeling arises because Hokusai has depicted the wave in what I would call "stop-action."

Waves move in a relentless chain. If the movement were to stop even for an instant, we would no longer have waves. Waves are not objects the way flowers or trees, much less mountains, are. Waves are motion itself. What Hokusai has done is to capture the wild motion of a wave in a single instant and present it to us as a "thing." It is as if the eyes of Hokusai, who died in 1849 at the end of the Edo period, possessed the precision that characterizes the cameras of modern Japan over a century later. It is as though Hokusai stopped that wave with a shutter speed of one-thousandth of a second. That is why the wave in the print produces a stop-action, or perhaps slow-motion, effect. By reducing the focus to just one wave and freezing its motion at one instant, Hokusai has captured the movement of waves as they break up the horizon and has conveyed the temporal connection between them.

But Hokusai's wave denies the spatial expansion that a Western poet like Baudelaire might have given it. He replaces the vague shape and movement of expansion with the precision of reduction. Careful scrutiny of the print suggests the image of a narrow valley between two mountains. Yet within that "valley" is captured all of the vastness and violent motion of the sea. Slow-motion filming is far better at capturing a sense of speed and power than is shooting something at its actual speed. This Hokusai amply demonstrated. It might be called "the aesthetic of reducing motion."

The reduction aspects we have discussed up until now have been primarily concerned with space. But the stop-action waves of Hokusai and the slow-motion gestures of Nō actors, which chop movement into small units, represent a temporal reduction

of movement. And the frozen poses (*mie*) used by Kabuki actors at moments of dramatic tension are also a kind of stop-action.

It is said that in the movements of the Nō stage, which have
been pared down and perfected over the course of nearly six hundred years, a mere step or two forward indicates determination,
while retreating just one pace indicates discouragement. To show
desperation, the actor will assume a motionless attitude. Indeed,
by standing motionless the actor demonstrates motion! Some have
suggested that this is like a top which when spinning at its fastest
appears not to be moving.

When the idea of Hokusai's wave, which captures the movement and temporal intervals of all waves by reducing them to
a single wave in a single instant, is applied to humans it becomes
kamae, "the assuming of an attitude," "attitude" meant here in
both its physical and psychological senses. This is the attitude
referred to in judo and Japanese fencing (*kendō*). It is not a difficult concept. In Japan, the concept of attitude appears in archery, flower arranging, tea ceremony, and all other traditional
arts. An attitude presents all action, be it movement that is about
to occur or movement that has already happened, in reduced
form. It is that single moment of action that contains both the
beginning and end of action. It is completely different from the
Western concepts of style and form, which treat all action as a
discreet unit. An attitude is not static. We can simply say that
Hokusai's wave print shows "the attitude of waves" because it
is stillness in motion.

In Japan, training or practice (*keiko*) in a particular art can
be thought of as the process of internalizing the attitude appropriate to that art. Professor Nakamura Hajime has suggested
that what distinguishes Japanese Buddhism from other forms of
Buddhism is its insistence that enlightenment can be achieved
in one lifetime, in the body one has now. In other words, as
the great thirteenth-century Zen monk Dōgen preached, it is not
the heart that is enlightened but the body. Dōgen said: "Strive

to rid yourself of your heart's cares and thoughts. Just sit in meditation and the Way will open up for you. If you do this, the Way will become one with your physical being. Remember that this is achieved solely by sitting in meditation, and work diligently at it." With these words Dōgen is saying that the sitting "attitude" is the very heart of Zen.

Japanese archery is no different. Dōgen said that with the right sitting attitude enlightenment would come naturally. In the same way, the Japanese archer is not concerned if his arrow misses the target. In fact, one of the peculiar characteristics of Japanese archery is that more attention is paid to whether the archer has assumed the proper shooting attitude than to anything else. The belief is that if the proper attitude is assumed the arrow will naturally fly to the target. This practice can even be seen in modern baseball. Robert Whiting, author of *The Chrysanthemum and the Bat* (New York: Dodd, Mead, 1977) has noted that while American batters are more concerned with results than with form or style, in Japan "a good player is one who can merge his own movements with correct form; everything else will follow in time."

The perfect model for "assuming an attitude" is to be found in Japanese fencing. This is what one of the top fencing masters, Satō Sadao, has to say on the subject in his book *Watakushi no kendō shūgyō* (*My Pursuit of Kendō*): "I begin by telling my students bluntly, 'You do not yet understand the concept of attitude.' " Satō goes on to say that an attitude is not merely the taking of a physical pose. The proper physical attitude can only be assumed when the psychological components of eagerness and willingness to make an effort are present. Once this is learned, body and spirit will of their own accord assume the proper attitude even when confronting one's opponent with a real sword rather than the bamboo one generally used. In other words, "assuming an attitude" really amounts to the concentration of the psyche.

Then Satō relates a story about the master swordsman and

painter Miyamoto Musashi (1584–1645). One day a young man with absolutely no understanding of the martial arts came to Musashi and begged to be instructed so that he could "single-handedly" avenge the death of his parents. Musashi took him at his word and literally taught him the use of the sword with one hand. But instead of teaching him fighting techniques, he simply taught him how to assume the proper attitude. When the son was ready to do battle, he sought out and insulted his parents' enemy, then proceeded to put on a blindfold. When he sensed his enraged opponent about to strike, he simply thrust out his sword and assumed the proper attitude. It was enough to fend off the attack. The enraged opponent began to slash out wildly. But there were no chinks in the young man's "attitude." With exactly two blows the son left his enemy fallen in a pool of red.

Attitude, the essence of Japanese swordsmanship, consists in contracting one's movements and one's spirit into a compact form. Satō concludes by noting that it is possible to tell a swordsman's level of ability simply by observing the attitude he assumes with his sword.

The concept of attitude can be found in daily life as well as the arts, and it manifests itself in individual and group behavior. It can be seen in the meticulous planning of responses to possible future occurrences, in the concentration of mental energies, and, in general, in the mental outlook of the Japanese. The word here is *kokorogamae*, which means "mental attitude" and suggests readiness or preparedness. It is precisely this quality that allowed the Japanese to dig their way out of the ashes of the Second World War and build themselves into the economic power they are today.

Bear in mind that "assuming an attitude" means reducing any number of actions to a single form and any length of time to a single moment. One might wonder, then, to what one facial expression an attitude appropriate to any sort of emotion could be reduced. The answer is this: the Nō mask.

All the peoples of the world have produced masks. Masks represent the face carried in the deepest recesses of a people's heart. If we can isolate what makes Japanese masks different from other masks, we should be able to discover the unique face of Japanese culture. One notable difference is that, like the other models of reduction we have examined so far, Japanese masks have gotten smaller over time yet are ever more completely realized. From the earliest Gigaku dance masks, with their exaggerated expressions, masks in Japan were gradually refined down to the Nō mask, with its neutral expression capable of portraying any feeling.

In other countries, masks have been fitted with devices so that they can change expression, or they have been given one fixed expression—anger, for example, or joy—to suit the emotions of a particular character type. But Japanese Nō masks, especially those used by the main character (*shite*), have reduced all emotions to a single neutral expression, in the same way that the swordsman reduces all his energies to a single attitude.

A look at the mouth of a Nō mask tells a great deal. Of the more than one hundred types of Nō mask, there are only two with tightly closed mouths. All the others have mouths that are half open, neutrally poised between being tightly closed and wide open. This type of expressionless face has spawned the phrase "a face like a Nō mask." Expressionless though it may seem, however, it is capable of expressing any emotion precisely because of its neutral quality. In a word, it is the facial equivalent of attitude. The same Nō mask, when tilted slightly downward in a movement called "clouding over," shows pathos but, when tilted slightly upward in a movement called "shining," shows joy or pleasure.

The frozen expression of the Nō mask, like the attitude of the master swordsman, carries in it the potential to move with just the slightest shift from a position of rest to any one of hundreds of expressions. It is the Japanese face itself.

This aspect of Japanese reductionism is not only to be seen on the Nō stage. The "Nō mask" of young women, which can change with the subtlest of movements, can be seen anywhere in Japan—on a street corner, in a hotel lobby, or in an international conference hall. The broadly smiling face, coupled with a deep bow, conveys all manner of emotions, including sincerity, politeness, kindness, delicacy, and so on. But as soon as this extended greeting is finished, the face returns to a cool, composed expression that is hard to reconcile with the one seen an instant before. In fact, this simply marks a return to the proper, neutral attitude—a point that foreigners often misunderstand.

Remember what so surprised Ruth Benedict, author of *The Chrysanthemum and the Sword*, and the rest of the world. After the Japanese defeat in the Second World War no one expected them to submit passively when the American army landed, for the face that the Japanese had shown until then had been that of the *kamikaze* pilots. Yet in the space of a morning that face had changed, and there were the Japanese kindly welcoming their visitors. It was an example of the Japanese ability to change course. Both faces were a surprise to the Western world, which knew nothing of the Nō mask and its reduction of all feelings into one form.

Hokusai's wave is not at rest. The stately gestures of Nō, which have been called "moving sculpture," may appear slow, but they are not really so. Despite appearances to the contrary, the basic attitude of Japanese fencing is not one of just standing rooted to the spot. And the Nō mask, which is carved in wood, is by no means frozen. These are all examples of the innate Japanese ability to change course. In the blink of an eye Hokusai's wave will break, the Nō actor's stamping foot will set off a shower of sparks, and the motionless sword will become a flash of lightning. The Nō mask will, with a slight tilt, convey even the most extreme of emotions; the proper attitude, with just a minor shift in line of sight, will become a concentrated gaze. And a concentrated gaze is what Bashō was writing about in the following *haiku*:

> If you look closely—
> The fence is blooming
> With *nazuna* flowers

"If you look closely" at this poem by Bashō, you will see that the brush-wielding poet assumes an attitude just as surely as does the sword-wielding samurai warrior. The Buddhist scholar D. T. Suzuki (1870–1966) compared this *haiku* to Tennyson's "Flower in the crannied wall" in order to examine differences in Eastern and Western ways of thinking. The very fact that he chose two short poems in order to compare East and West is evidence of the Japanese tendency toward reductionism. But that aside, it would be far better to say that Bashō's poem shows specifically Japanese characteristics rather than broadly Eastern ones. Had Professor Suzuki forgotten that *Korea's* representative poetic form is the *sijo*, not the *haiku*, and that the Bashō of that form was Yun Sŏndo? He would perhaps not otherwise have picked Bashō's *haiku* to represent all of East Asia, for Yun's poetry is as different from Bashō's as Bashō's is from Tennyson's.

This is Tennyson's poem:

> Flower in the crannied wall,
> I pluck you out of the crannies,
> I hold you here, root and all, in my hand,
> Little flower—but *if* I could understand
> What you are, root and all, and all in all,
> I should know what God and man is.

Certainly the Tennyson poem Professor Suzuki chose is characteristically European. As he notes, "Bashō did not pick the flower, he just stared at it intently," but "Tennyson cruelly plucked the flower from the place where it was growing; he removed the flower from the earth that nurtures it." Tennyson was active, while Bashō was contemplative and not inclined to disturb things. Whereas Bashō reacted with surprise and wonder, Tennyson posed hypotheses as though to get at the truth of the mysteries lying behind God and man. This, at least, is how Professor Suzuki compares these two poems.

Now let's introduce one of Yun's poems:

> Fog lifts from the cove.
> The mountains behind brighten with sun.
> At night the tide ebbs,
> In daytime it comes in.
> Flowers round the river village—
> Much better when seen from afar.

Yun sees these flowers in a way different from both Tennyson and Bashō. He does not behave like Tennyson. He does not pick the flowers he sees and subject them to a botanist's analysis. In this he is Eastern and like Bashō. Yet nor does he try to "look closely" at the flowers as Bashō does. He consciously rejects close scrutiny, as is clear from his line "Much better when seen from afar." Bashō draws close to his flower with the intention of staring at it intently. In fact, in the intensity of his scrutiny he is doing much the same as Tennyson, that is, examining the flower from the roots up. Yun, on the other hand, renounces any attempt to get closer to his flowers or examine them carefully. From his standpoint, there is no difference between the behavior of Tennyson and that of Bashō. While they both seek to get closer to the flowers, he wants to get as far away from them as possible. He does not stare at his flowers intently; he sees them indistinctly, from a distance, for he feels that is when the flowers are at their most beautiful. When the human viewpoint does not intrude, nature shows itself as it truly is. This, surely, is the contemplative stance that distinguishes East from West.

Bashō, too, had started out looking at nature in a vague sort of way. He had been enjoying the spring scenery before he "looked closely" at the flower. Yet it was not enough to look at the scene around him.

Family Crests—Congealing

Sight and hearing are the most important of the five senses to our cultural activity. Civilization is built on things seen and things heard. I would like to suggest here that the visual sense tends toward contraction but the auditory sense toward expansion.

In Japanese, it is possible to concentrate or pack in (*tsumeru*) seeing (*miru*) and come up with the compound word meaning "to stare," *mitsumeru*. But there is no such compound for hearing. Sound travels outward in waves and becomes inaudible after a certain length of time. It is practically impossible to contract sound waves artificially. But with things seen, the seer can control space and exercise his own volition to contract what is seen.

Earlier we examined how the poet Issa looked at the Milky Way not in its enormous, expansive fullness but through a tiny hole in the paper screen door. His poem ("How beautiful! / Through a hole in the paper screen / I can see the Milky Way") came into being when he contracted the broad night sky and its Milky Way by means of a little tear in the screen. With sound, however, although we can stop up our ears and block it out, we cannot contract it. Even when heard through a hole in a paper screen a waterfall does not sound like insects chirping in the grass.

Engelbert Kaempfer, at the turn of the seventeenth century, was lavish in his praise of Japanese painting, yet he was silent on the subject of Japanese music. His compatriot, the German Philipp Franz von Siebold, who came to Japan in the early 1820s to practice medicine at the Dutch mission in Nagasaki as Kaempfer had many years before, respected painting most among all the arts of Japan but felt that Japanese music was not very highly developed. In this respect, it is interesting to note that the technique of synaesthesia, the confusion of senses, is often found in Japanese literature, where sounds are sometimes "seen." These two *haiku*, the first by Bashō and the second by Buson, illustrate the point:

Dusk falls on the sea—
Calls of ducks
Sound faintly white.

Here in the stable
Mosquitoes buzz darkly
In lingering summer heat.

Haiku poets frequently attribute the qualities of light and color to sounds. In perhaps his most famous poem, while he does not actually use synaesthesia, Bashō does make sound visible to the eye. A literal translation makes the point best:

Furu ike ya	Old pond!
Kawazu tobikomu	A frog jumps in—
Mizu no oto	Sound of water.

The "sound of water," even the slightest murmuring of a brook, is by definition expansive. The English expression "sound of water" implies flowing water, a running stream or brook, and it fails to convey the soft splash of Bashō's frog jumping into the pond. This is why R. H. Blyth chose to substitute the onomatopoeic "plop" for the last line of his translation: "The old pond / A frog jumps in— / Plop!"

Bashō envelopes his "sound of water" with three visual images: an old pond, a frog, and a leap. And without resorting to onomatopoeia, he nonetheless manages to reduce the scale of the sound. His poem has a setting and time represented by the old pond. It has a character, the frog, and a plot, the frog's leap. In other words, in seventeen syllables he has given us the three essential elements of a novel or a play. In this way the theme and central image—the sound of water—becomes more than a mere auditory phenomenon.

Modern *haiku* follow this pattern too. This is one of Mizuhara Shūōshi's poems:

> Into the lapis blue marsh
> Falls a cascade of water
> That turns to lapis blue.

He says nothing about the sound of the cascade; instead, he portrays the visual sensation of its whiteness falling into the marsh and turning greenish blue. This poet is not listening to the waterfall, he is staring at it intently.

But the Japanese do not stop at giving sounds color, that is to say, turning something audible into something visual. They also have a tendency to give visual form to words and to other abstractions. For example, *The Genji Scroll* gives a full and rich visual account of the *Tale of Genji*. Often a verse alone was not enough for the *haiku* poet, so he would paint a simple picture, called a *haiga*, to go with it. This translating of words into pictures is a kind of congealing of the abstract, an attempt to turn the abstract into something concrete. That the Japanese have this tendency shows even in their approach to Buddhism. They have not produced much in the way of commentaries on the sutras or abstract theology. Rather, they have constructed a Buddhism out of temples, monasteries, Buddhist statuary, and meditation gardens.

This reductive process involving the congealing of ideas is seen most clearly in the Japanese family crest, in which the vagueness of history and the Japanese sense of group consciousness are given concrete and visible form. Traditionally in Korea not even the royal family had a family crest or coat-of-arms. It is true that the Yi dynasty (1392–1910) was represented by a crest depicting a pear blossom, but it was a late development and possibly influenced by Japanese practices. In China too, although dragons and the like were used as symbols of the throne, there was nothing like a family crest. Japan is another matter. In terms of history, variety, design, and significance, Japanese family crests are comparable to those of Europe.

In the *Buke jiki* (*History of the Warrior Houses*), Yamaga Sokō (1622–85), pioneer in the study of family crests, maintains that they "began with Shōtoku Taishi" (574–622), and came to be used by various families as a family mark "from the time of Yoritomo" (Minamoto no Yoritomo, 1147–99, founder of the Kamakura shogunate). The great scholar and official Arai Hakuseki (1657–1725) also traces the development of family crests in his book *Shinsho* (*Guide to the Aristocracy*). He claims that sometime in the late Heian period (794–1184) the nobility began to put marks on their carts and these marks became family crests. But what interests us here is not whether the family crest arose as a mark on a suit of armor to distinguish ally from enemy on the battlefield or whether it originally functioned like today's automobile license plates. Nor is it important when the family crest first came to be widely used. The real question is why, by the middle of the Edo period in the eighteenth century, there were twelve thousand different types of family crests being used in Japan, and not just by the nobility but by urban merchants, farmers, and even courtesans. Even in the 1980s crests are still a source of interest. In October of 1981, the Japan Local Saké Distillers Cooperative Distribution Association came out with a new brand of saké for use on ceremonial occasions. It is called "Family Crest Saké," and its label features 664 family crests, a figure that represents ninety-five percent of the crests in use in Japan today.

It has been argued that family crests are a product of societies in which reverence is shown to the family ancestors, but this is a contention that requires some examination. Traditional Korean society practiced a Confucian orthodoxy in which respect for family lineage and one's ancestors was more pronounced than in Japan. Yet the Koreans never developed family crests. In Japan one pays homage only to those immediate ancestors who remain in one's memory, but in Korea formal respect is paid to all ancestors, never mind whether they lived countless generations back in the distant past. The Koreans did not normally use family crests; instead, they kept family genealogies in which the names of ancestors were carefully recorded.

The fact that the Japanese showed respect for their ancestors through the family crest whereas the Koreans used family genealogies for the same purpose does tell us something about the differences between the two cultures. The family genealogy is a systematic way of showing a family's history. It records and preserves a lineage in much the same way as the modern family register does. As is to be expected in a traditional society dominated by literati, the genealogy is conceptual and in written form. The family crest, on the other hand, shows the sense of history and group in concrete form. It is not a system; it is a symbolic image. Unlike the genealogy, the family crest is not in a written form that can be preserved and stored on a bookshelf. It is something that is to be waved like a flag in front of one and all. Thus an abstract group affiliation is congealed through the use of a family crest into a concrete form.

In a culture where family genealogies are the rule, discussion revolves around who you are descended from and the name elements used to distinguish the various generations. But in a culture that uses family crests, names play a different role in the family history. Japanese can change their family names with ease and a clear conscience. In the old days, when a wife entered her husband's home she would change her surname but rarely her family crest.

More than anything else, the family crest differs from the family genealogy in that even a quick glance at a crest produces a sensory reaction. The paulownia crest of Hideyoshi immediately conveys the brief splendor and sudden fall of the Toyotomi family. The three-leafed hollyhock crest of the Tokugawa family calls to mind the implacable power of the shoguns who ruled Japan for over two and a half centuries. And the sixteen-petaled, eightfold chrysanthemum crest of the Japanese imperial family represents to some the sacred divinity of the emperors and to others the militarism of the recent past.

The family crest decorates everything from clothes, gate, and house to saké cups and paper lanterns, and it etches itself deeply in people's minds. Its symbolic design comes to elicit a conditioned response, brought unconsciously to the point of parody in period dramas, where a glance at the hero's family crest sends people reeling back in awe in recognition of the power of his clan. Thus a family crest is more than a mark of family lineage; it is a public symbol of that family itself.

Seen in this light, the crest becomes more important than the actual family. This sounds less far-fetched if one thinks of the Christian cross. The theology, history, and community of Christianity are too diffuse to be easily grasped. But when expressed with a single symbol they become readily accessible. Consider the number of martyrs who "died for the cross." In the secular world the flag performs the same function. Modern nation states use the flag and other such symbols to rally their own people and to display their authority to the rest of the world. In Japan the family crest instilled in members of the family, and even in retainers who were not related by blood, an almost religious loyalty and sense of group identity.

Just as the family crest symbolized the honor and group consciousness of a particular house, so the short jacket (*hanten*) performed a similar function for workers and artisans. The short jacket is thought to have been a modification of the *manteau* introduced from Portugal. In addition to being a work jacket, it bore identification markings which publicly displayed the group to which the wearer belonged. If the family crest was a symbol of pride in one's bloodline and family history, the short jacket and its insignia represented the worker's skills and pride in his occupation. The huge insignia dyed on the back of the short jacket announced to the world the wearer's affiliations and meant that his individual actions immediately reflected on the group to which he belonged.

In the world of commerce the short jacket's function was—and still is—performed by the shop curtain (*noren*) that hangs over the entrance to the establishment. Like the short jacket, the shop curtain performed two functions: to protect the shop from sun and wind and to display the shop's logo. Merchants worked—and tried to establish customer trust—"for the sake of the shop curtain." If a shop burnt down, the shop curtain was saved at any cost; it was not just some dirty old rag.

In modern times the crests of such families as the Mitsui and the Iwasaki, founders of Mitsubishi, have become the logos for giant companies. They have become little badges which each employee wears on his or her lapel. And they have become the trademarks that companies like National put on every one of their products. Today's company employees follow in the tradition of the warriors who fought for their family crest, of the artisans who carved and crafted for the sake of the insignia on their short jackets, and of the merchants who sought to foster a reputation for reliability in order to preserve the honor of their shop curtain. For Japanese there is no escaping from this crest-dominated life; it lies at the heart of Japanese groupism. It is impossible to live apart from the group. The Japanese feel an unbearable sense of insecurity if left alone. But once they have entered a group and come under the auspices of a crest, the sense of relief is immense. Even when they go abroad, they file in behind the flag, the flag held aloft by the tour group leader.

The crest depicts allegiance to a group but affords no inkling of rank within the group. This vital role is performed by one of the most familiar accoutrements of life in Japan, the business or name card (*meishi*). In Japan, your business life is as much dependent on the business card as your daily life is on food. My own first embarrassments in Japan occurred during my first week in the country, a whole crucial week without business cards. Until they were ready, meeting people was a nightmare. To meet someone face-to-face is never sufficient. The name card in Japanese business is like the gun in a Western movie—drawn before questions are asked. A slow draw means, if not death, at least much loss of face. A quick draw, however, must be followed by a slow stare at the card and an appraisal of its contents.

At a meeting, therefore, the face—the reduced face—presented on a person's business card is more important than that person's real face. But let's be more anatomically accurate—it is not the face of the card but the shoulder, the corner, that is important, for this is where the pertinent information regarding occupation, rank, and suchlike is written.

The crux of the matter lies here. It is an issue of primary importance to adopt the proper facial expression when reading the "shoulder" of a business card. Your face must be grave, but with just a slight look of surprise and a faint nod of approval (bearing in mind that the more important the person the more emphatic the nod). Then you must put the card respectfully in your pocket as though it were an article of great importance. Anyone who just snatches the business card and, without looking at it, pops it into his pocket as if it were a wrinkled old handkerchief is not abiding by the rules of the game.

In Japan, land of the family crest, the belief is that you do not really know someone until you have seen his business card. Just looking at his face is not enough. Because business cards are trusted, more perhaps than facial expressions, a vast business is done in fraudulent cards—or at least misleading ones.

Business cards, however, did not originate in Japan. The practice of using business cards is thought to have been introduced a little more than a century ago when a mission sent to the United States by the shogun returned to Japan. The history of business cards in Japan is not, therefore, very old. But its lack of age is made up for by an excess of affection. The Japanese fondness for business cards stems, as I see it, from the tendency to make things smaller. In this way, a wide, abstract world is reduced to a manageable form. On one little card everything one needs to know about the other person is displayed: his group affiliation, his rank in that group, his address, and his telephone number. A whole human life is shrunk down to a 5.5 by 9 centimeter card. That is why, when two people meet in Japan, they scrutinize each other's business card first and face second. The business card, in its reduction and its transferal of individual personality onto a piece of paper, exemplifies yet again the Japanese tendency to contract or reduce things.

We have by now examined six examples of Japanese reductionism. But objects like the folding fan or the *anesama* doll are finished products. They have already been reduced. However, since reduction is a process, we must look at verbs in order to understand it more fully. Interpretations of Japan have tended to focus on various specific concepts, but in seeking to encapsulate Japanese culture into one or two concepts, the authors of these interpretations themselves fall victim to the Japanese tendency toward reduction. The very title of that classic interpretation, Ruth Benedict's *The Chrysanthemum and the Sword*, speaks for this approach. But if we really feel a need to sum up Japan in a catch-phrase (which, after all, is what I am trying to do here), a verb ought to be more appropriate than a noun. A noun is too static for this purpose; verbs, however, are always moving, always changing, like a wave. This is why each of the six models of reductionism we examined earlier was expressed in terms of a verb. The verb "reduce" is itself dynamic, so we have used active verbs to describe each type of reduction, including: folding, holding, and bringing closer; taking away and paring down; packing in; assuming an attitude; and congealing. Whether they be performed to improve the quality of an object or to satisfy the psyche, for aesthetic reasons or to make an object more concrete and functional, these actions each contribute to the creation of a culture.

3

THE CULTURE OF REDUCTION-ISM AS MANIFESTED IN NATURE

Ropes and Wheels

Since ancient times, the Japanese have dreamt of bringing the vastness of nature into their own homes. Witness the following lines of a poem from the *Man'yōshū*: "Though I would stretch a rope / To pull the peak of Tago closer. . . ." When the imagery of the poet is applied to actual, everyday life, what we get is the Japanese garden.

The Koreans, unlike the Japanese, tend to go out and see nature on its own terms rather than try to bring it in closer to themselves. Yi Kyubo, a Korean poet of the Koryŏ dynasty, wrote verses comparing the beauty of his lover to a mountain just as did the anonymous *Man'yōshū* poet cited above. Yi thought, however, not in terms of a rope, but a wheel. He imagined riding around the base of a nearby mountain in an open four-wheel carriage pulled by his servants, while he played the zither and enjoyed the scenery.

This approach is unlikely to give rise to the kind of gardens the Japanese created. Korean literati, including Zen priests, did not regard nature as something to be beckoned, brought into their houses, and closed up. They saw it as something they must leave their homes for and go out to see. For that they needed wheels, not a rope. They were not interested in gardens. Their ideal was to go out to the soaring mountains and flowing rivers and see them in their own element. Thus the representative image is of an open viewing carriage, its four walls taken away so that the

scenery can be enjoyed on all sides. The Korean literati loved viewing-towers and viewing-pavilions, and such structures were built wherever a beautiful mountain or river could be seen and enjoyed. A poem by the modern Korean poet Kim Sowŏl illustrates my point:

> Mother, sister, let's live by the river.
> Before us the glittering silver of sand;
> Behind us the whispering wind through reeds.
> Mother, sister, let's live by the river.

The glittering sand and the whispering of the wind through the reeds beckon the poet to leave his home, to leave the house where he lives now and build a new one by the river. What the poet seeks to change is not nature itself but his dwelling place, so that he may be closer to nature. In this context, constructing a garden does not mean making a prisoner of nature by bringing it into one's home. It means building a house in the middle of nature or a hut deep in the mountains.

When the critic Yoshimura Teiji came to Korea, he visited the Secret Garden in Seoul. His remarks reveal a great deal about the different views of nature held by Japanese and Koreans:

> I visited the Secret Garden in Seoul. It was located on a low hill thickly covered with a variety of trees just sending out new green leaves. As I walked around this famous area, I soon forgot I was walking in a garden. The hill had been left untouched, and it was too much a natural forest. . . . It seemed to me like the setting of a garden before the garden has been put in. Beautiful though the hillside scenery may have been, it was not a garden. Anyway, that's how I, as a Japanese, felt. [From *Chinmoku no Nihon-bi* (*The Japanese Beauty of Silence*), Tokyo: Mainichi Shinbunsha, 1974.]

Whatever his intentions, Yoshimura has written perhaps the highest possible praise of the Secret Garden, or any other Korean garden for that matter. Why? Because the illusion that the Secret Garden is not a garden but nature left to itself is precisely what the creators of the garden were striving for. Before Korea came under the influence of Japanese ideas about gardening, there was no pruning or arranging of trees. So natural does the Secret Garden appear that Japanese tourists have been known to ask passers-by, "Where on earth is that famous Secret Garden?" And this while they are standing right in the middle of it!

The Japanese prefer to pull the mountain peak to themselves with a rope. Japan is the land where festival goers will carry around a two-ton replica of Mount Fuji at the Fuji Yoshida fire festival. It is the land where people took a gigantic rock, eight meters high and twenty-three meters in circumference, from the Inland Sea, broke it into some ninety pieces, carried it to Kō-rakuen garden in Okayama and reconstructed it there. Even the largest gardens of the feudal lords, gardens like Kōrakuen, are nature controlled by the human hand.

Despite their shared religious outlook, Korean Zen Buddhists and Japanese Zen Buddhists reflect this same difference in their approach to nature. Korean Zen monks performed their religious activities in places far removed from the daily world. Monks like Choui of the late Yi dynasty, who wandered through the mountains, sometimes settling long enough to build and occupy a tiny hut before moving on, preferred to meet nature face-to-face and sought to become one with it.

On the other hand, Japanese Zen monks tended to gather in the midst of the throng; they sought to bring nature to them. This approach can be seen in the "abbot's garden" found in most Zen temples. Unlike Chinese or Korean Zen masters, Japanese Zen masters were not interested in contemplating the cosmos by immersing themselves in nature untrammeled. They contemplated the eternal and boundless void by gazing at small gardens of stones and sand—the stones representing mountains, sand symbolizing the sea—gardens that were laid out right there beside the veranda.

The Japanese would not feel at home with the sentiment expressed in the following lines of a Korean poem: "Mountains, rivers—they cannot be carried home / So let us gaze upon them as they are, encircling us." Nor is theirs the power found in the Chinese idiom "Strong enough to uproot mountains." No—the Japanese, using their unique imagination and their skill at reducing what is found in nature, would pull with their metaphorical rope mountains and sea into their tiny gardens. But before one can pull the vastness of nature into the narrow confines of a garden, one must first contract it, make it smaller. Japanese garden designers have, over the centuries, devised several methods of contracting nature. One of the most prominent of these, and one that bears resemblance to the Chinese and Korean approach, is the "borrowed scenery" (shakkei) technique.

The concept of borrowed scenery is expressed in a line by the Chinese poet Tao Yuanming (?–427): "I pluck a chrysanthemum and gaze off at the Southern Mountains." The scenery beyond is a background for, and an integral part of, one's own garden. This idea is certainly not unique to Japan. It can be found in China and in gardens in Britain too. But Japanese principles of borrowed scenery, which were more or less fixed by the fifteenth century, went beyond a simple use of the surroundings, as expressed by Nishizawa Fumitaka: "Borrow the mountains. Borrow waters. Borrow the billowing clouds. When flowers are in season, borrow flowers. When snow is in season, borrow snow" (Teien-ron I [A Discussion of Gardens], vol. 1, Tokyo: Sagami Shobō, 1975). What is borrowed becomes the main element of the garden. In Japan, borrowed scenery is a much more actively applied technique than it is elsewhere. Mount Hiei, the borrowed feature of the well-known garden at Entsū Temple in the suburbs of Kyoto, is more than just a backdrop for the garden.

Yet at the same time, the garden is not just an observation deck for viewing the mountain. Towering Mount Hiei exists right there in the garden itself. The garden acts like a rope and pulls the mountain in so that it becomes an organic part of the scene.

In functional terms, the feature borrowed for a borrowed scenery garden dictates the aesthetics and layout of that garden. If the trees in the garden are too tall they will block the view of the mountain borrowed for the garden. If, on the other hand, they are too short, the middle ground between the garden and the mountain will be visible, and the seamless joining of the two will be compromised. What matters most with the borrowed view is that there be no obstructions on the one hand and yet that it not be too intrusive on the other. This means inevitably that the trees in the garden cannot be allowed to grow as they would naturally. At this point the human consciousness enters into the picture, taking a hand in the height, placement, and distribution of the trees. In order that the borrowed mountain and the garden appear to be joined as one, a fence is put up around the garden; and the arrangement of the rocks, the pruning of the shrubbery, even the shape of the garden are all done in such a way as to integrate the borrowed view. The tension in the relationships between these elements is essential to the success of the composition.

Yoshimura Teiji maintains that the uniqueness of the garden at Entsū Temple lies in the fact that it is laid out so that the borrowed scenery makes the garden appear smaller than it actually is. The distribution of the rocks, the trees, and the moss keeps the boundaries of the garden in check, and "works to concentrate the space of the garden." Thus, says Yoshimura, "the condensed space of the garden acts as a lens to show off Mount Hiei in all its beauty, all its majesty, all its expansiveness" (*Niwa: Nihon-bi no sōzō* [*Gardens: Creations of the Japanese Aesthetic*], Tokyo: Rokkō Shuppan, 1981).

Let's take another look at that prototype of Japanese aesthetics, the folding fan. When open, all the ribs of the fan are gathered at one point, the pivot, which is held in the hand. The closer one gets to the pivot, the closer together are the ribs. The edge of the fan is spread out and it gets smaller as one moves towards the center. Mount Hiei is the edge of the fan. The countless lines of sight, which serve as "ropes" to pull the mountain into the garden, are the ribs of the fan. And the pivot that holds everything together and provides the power to pull everything inward, like the pivot of the fan, is the garden of Entsū Temple itself.

The Garden as Picture Scroll

The "contracted scenery" (*shukkei*) garden, a kind of garden featuring a scaled-down version of some famous natural landscape, is an even more active and direct expression of the principle of making nature one's own property. Rather than borrow a natural feature, the contracted scenery garden copies it on a smaller scale. Though the term normally calls to mind the gardens of the feudal lords of the Edo period (1603–1868), the contracted scenery garden has a history as old as Japanese gardening itself.

In the Asuka (552–646) and Nara (646–794) periods, gardens were called "islands" (*shima*). The following poem from the *Man'yōshū* is an early example of this use of the term:

The island we planted,
My beloved and I—
Its trees are now tall,
Its foliage lush!

Soga no Umako (?–626), head of the powerful Soga clan, constructed a large garden for which he became known as the Island Lord. The remains of what might well have been his garden have recently been excavated at a place known as Shima (Island) on the site of the old capital of Asuka at the southern end of the Nara Plain. Judging from this use of the word island, it would seem that these ancient gardens were scaled-down models of sea and island scenery.

Scholars of the history of gardens have posited several interesting theories as to why the Japanese chose to bring seascapes into their inland gardens. The most plausible concerns the fact that in the Asuka and Nara periods Japanese travelers on missions to China or to western Japan sailed through the Inland Sea. After a long return sea voyage they were greeted by its beautiful seascapes, and this made them want to preserve the memory by reconstructing its scenery in the form of "islands," that is to say, gardens, in their homes in Nara.

Other theories have been proposed to explain the phenomenon. One suggests that, because Japan is an archipelago inhabited by migrants, its inhabitants have retained a fondness for maritime scenery even when living inland. Another supposes that the early garden seascapes were for the ancients a representation of an ideal land that lay beyond the seas. Each of these theories has its faults, but one thing we are sure of is that Asuka and Nara period gardens were reduced representations of seascapes. These early gardens consisted of a pond with an island in the middle. At the water's edge white sand or tiny pebbles were spread to form a beach, beside which pine trees were planted. These were not ordinary seascapes. Contracted scenery gardens copied, on a reduced scale, particular locations. In the ninth or tenth century, the Kawara-no-in garden (in Kyoto) was constructed in imitation of the salt kilns at Shiogama, a coastal village over seven hundred kilometers to the northeast. And Sumiyoshi beach in Osaka Prefecture was rendered in reduced form in a garden of one of the aristocratic Taira clan in Kyoto.

By the Edo period, all the major feudal lords had their own large gardens. But these strolling gardens (kaiyūshiki teien) were not displays of nature in its natural state. They were all "nature contracted," for their origins were in the small tea gardens built by the tea masters. And the basis of these large gardens was the contracted scenery technique. Okazaki Fumiaki describes how the feudal lords got the idea for the scenery in their gardens:

> The feudal lords of the Edo period were required to divide their time between Edo and the region over which they had administrative jurisdiction. Impressed by the scenery they saw on their trips back and forth, they reduced these scenes in scale and reproduced them along the pathways of their gardens. The Toyama-sō garden in Tokyo and the Suizen Temple garden in Kumamoto are fine examples of this.

No matter how large these gardens were, they were but scaled down versions of the original scenery. As the Edo period progressed, the building of artificial miniature mountains became popular. These mountains were usually copies of real mountains such as Mount Fuji, which is thought to have been the model for the artificial mountain in the Suizen Temple garden mentioned by Okazaki above.

The book *Nihon no niwa, 7 (Japanese Gardens*, vol. 7, by Itō Teiji et al., Tokyo: Shōgakukan, 1978), discusses how these gardens should be appreciated. It gives as an example a garden that features a model scene of the Sumiyoshi Pine, a pine tree famous for its longevity and legendary associations:

> It is not simply a matter of appreciating the wonders of the pine tree's shape. By looking at the model pine, all of the associations of the real Sumiyoshi Pine—the poems composed about it, the pictures painted of it—are conjured up, and the mind forms an image of that famous shoreline.

The borrowed scenery technique brings into the garden something that can actually be seen from where one is standing.

The contracted scenery technique pulls some distant scene into the garden. Be it Mount Fuji, the Kiso Valley, the Tatsuta River, or the beach at Waka, the contracted scenery garden reproduces these famous spots as though they were depicted on a picture scroll spread out before the viewer's eyes. Even scenery from other countries has found its way into Japanese gardens—the West Lake of Hangzhou in China, for example, which reappears at Kōrakuen in Tokyo's Koishikawa.

It is as if the painters of old turned to garden designing and fitted their scenes into the confines of a garden as they would fit them into a frame. Just as the *Tale of Genji* became a famous picture scroll, so the strolling garden at the Katsura Detached Palace in Kyoto is a "tale of scenery" depicted with trees and rocks. Walking down the seven hundred meters of paths in the Katsura garden is like walking down a road for hundreds of kilometers. Seen from the teahouse known as the Shōkintei, the garden presents a great seascape. But viewed from the Shōkatei, the scene is of a hidden valley deep in the mountains, while from a bay window on the south side of the Shōiken, one sees a plain of rice fields. This garden expresses in the reduced space of perhaps three or four hectares the vastly different aspects of sea, mountain, and plain.

In a contracted scenery garden, a pine tree is a pine tree, but at the same time it is a reduction of some greater, more complex natural scene and all the associations that scene conveys. A pine tree in a garden of this kind, therefore, is different from pine trees in nature. A thousand pine trees, the sea, the waves, the salt breeze, the white sand on the weather-beaten shore—all these images are reduced to the gnarled branches of the single pine tree in the garden. The garden pine is made a symbol for all of nature.

Both the borrowed and contracted scenery styles of garden came originally from the Asian continent. A story in the *Nihon shoki* relates how Empress Suiko employed Korean artisans to build a garden featuring a replica of the legendary Mount Sumeru, the central axis of the universe in Buddhist cosmology. But the change from the continental style to a purely Japanese style of garden was made possible by the emergence of the reduction principle. The Heian period (794–1184) is more closely associated with small gardens interspersed between the various buildings of a residence than with the larger-scale gardens built around a spring and a pond, although both styles are to be found in the gardens of that age.

When one sets about making nature smaller, rocks—not trees or water—are the most important element. It is the rocks that dictate the shape, movement, and space of trees and water. The grouping of rocks makes the reduced garden possible. Trees keep growing; water overflows or dries up. They are like human flesh. But rocks are like bone. A skeleton of rocks makes it possible to compress nature into a smaller space and bring it into the garden.

According to both the Heian period *Senzai hishō* (*Selected Secrets of Gardening*), which is the basic text of Japanese garden design, and the *Sakuteiki* (*Records of Garden Construction*), attributed to Tachibana no Toshitsuna (1028–94), the essence of gardening lies in the way the rocks are arranged. A garden is a nature poem painted with words of rock. By means of the rhetoric of rock grouping and placement, nature is simplified and reduced to a *haiku* garden. The Edo period aesthetic of contracted scenery gardens was vividly described centuries earlier in the following words from the *Sakuteiki*: "Imagine all the famous scenic spots in the various provinces. The most striking of these places can be made one's own. The greatest spectacles should be imitated in the garden in a way that will make them more intimate for us." One arranges rocks so as to copy the scenery of some famous place, but one reduces it in scale and makes it one's own. The central theme of the *Sakuteiki* is that "there are many ways to arrange rocks—to represent the sea, a great river, a mountain stream, marshland, rushes." And the work describes in exhaustive detail how rocks should be arranged to achieve these effects.

Arranging rocks is a way of contracting nature—the sea, mountain rivers, everything. Trees and water are only secondary to this process of reduction. But how does one go about making a reduced model of the sea using rocks? Tachibana no Toshitsuna explains: "To represent the sea you must start by arranging rocks in imitation of the surf-pounded crags of a beach." To express the sea, with its vast horizon, the gardener must begin by reducing it, as Takuboku did, down to the beach of a small island. If he can reproduce the image of rough crags weathered by the waves, it will be easy for people to imagine the great sea itself. Even without water or trees, the gardener can produce the effect of undulating waves and sea breezes through rocks alone.

Rocks can also be used to create the illusion of a great river. What gives movement to the flow of water is not the water itself. A river's snaking, twisting course is dictated by the rocks and other obstacles that block it here, guide it there. Thus, the *Sakuteiki* tells us, the powerful and relentless flow of water can be summoned up in the imagination simply through the skillful arrangement of rocks, regardless of whether there is but a trickle of water in one's garden or indeed no water at all. If there are many rocks on the bank, the river is narrow and its flow is swift. Fewer rocks, on the other hand, mean a wider river with a lazy flow.

Rocks are the nouns and verbs of the garden; trees and water are merely adjectives and adverbs. This is the grammar of a garden.

Dry Landscape—The Beautiful Captive

The use of rocks to depict natural scenery led eventually to that peculiarly Japanese creation, the dry landscape, which dispenses with the traditional elements of a garden and is composed solely of sand and rocks, thus further condensing nature.

In the dry landscape, making nature smaller depends not on copying some actual natural phenomenon on a reduced scale. Instead, a different process occurs. By paring, eliminating, cutting, peeling, and throwing away, a natural form not unlike a protoplasm results. Pare down and pare down some more. Discard the useless, the decorative. Peel away the layers that lie on nature as you would peel an onion. This reductive aesthetic runs exactly counter to the expansive quality of nature. It also implies removing nature from its tenuous existence in the shadow of time.

This aesthetic dictates that grass, which is weak and easily engulfed by time, must be the first to go. Trees and flowers, which the hand of the seasons sets trembling, must be cut away too. Even water must be excluded, for in its yielding nature it is expansive and marks the flow of time. And last we must exclude the earth, too, because it is eroded by time. Precipitous valley walls must be flattened out, and all returned to a perfectly horizontal plane.

All that is left after this crystallization of nature are a few hard rocks and some white sand. Just as the world is condensed into a few words in a *haiku*, so the movement of nature is reduced to and contained in rocks and sand. This is a space that human beings cannot enter. Expansion is absolutely forbidden. Beasts cannot walk nor birds fly through this world. Even sounds fade away here. Bashō wrote:

> The cicadas' shrill
> Sinks deep into the rocks—
> Perfect silence.

Similarly, all we can see in the dry landscape garden are the silent rocks and sand which soon absorb all sound. If a shrub nearby sprouts branches, these are quickly cut off, for they represent growth, expansion. In this concentrated environment a tree hardens like a fossil, just as water crystallizes into grains of sand.

But what happened to the nature that was there before the garden, or to time that passed too close to it? Perhaps they have been absorbed into unyielding rocks, or perhaps they are dancing around in the tense spaces between the carefully arranged stones. Though there are no trees, one sees a densely wooded mountain. Though there is no water, one sees a turbulent cascade. And in the narrow lines left by the rake in the sand appears the sea, frozen in time. The boundless world of nature is here in compact, condensed form. There is neither growth nor decay in this spatially expressed moment. And for the first time, our eyes are opened to the significance of the dry landscape.

The rock garden at Daisen-in, a sub-temple of Kyoto's Daitoku Temple, is a mere one hundred meters square. Yet the carefully selected rocks present a vision of nature much larger than that seen at bigger gardens such as the Katsura or Shūgaku-in detached palaces. Its expansive cosmic space holds a waterfall, a river, a body of water like the sea. And all of this is contracted into a small area by the painstaking grouping of rocks.

The garden designer Tessen Sōki was not exaggerating when he said:

> The five peaks tower high above, though they are no bigger than ant hills. The ocean looms vast, though it is no larger than the hole a frog lives in. Anything can be made to seem large by being made small. Within the boundaries of the garden, near and far disappear. A thousand miles is shrunk down to one foot. [From *Kasenzui no fu* (*An Informal Album of Landscaping*).]

The writer Shiga Naoya (1883–1971) spoke of the grammar of reductionism when he wrote of his reactions to the rock garden at Ryōan Temple:

Perhaps the fact that there is not a single tree nor a single blade of grass in the garden may seem somehow striking or mannered. But there is nothing striking or mannered about this garden. Surely the uniqueness of the approach adopted by Sōami [traditionally held to be the designer] lies in the way the vastness of nature is condensed into a garden a mere 165 meters square. [From *Ryōan-ji no niwa (The Garden of Ryōan Temple)*.]

Nature that has been pulled into the garden as a dry landscape is no longer the nature of the outside world. It has been pared down, simplified to the extreme, and brought up to the veranda. It is a special kind of nature that exists on its own terms apart from what we usually call nature.

Let us consider for a moment the Japanese word for a garden, *niwa*. Differing interpretations of its etymology exist, but they all agree that the word originally referred to something other than nature in its untrammeled state and that it designated a space in which some sort of human activity was carried out. There is one theory which holds that the word *niwa* is a corrupted and abbreviated form of a phrase meaning "a place that makes one smile when one sees it." Farfetched though this may sound, there is a certain nice aptness to it. A garden *is* a space that makes one smile when one sees it. Another clue in our quest for a better understanding of the concept of *niwa* is provided by the word *niwatori*, which literally means a "garden bird"—in other words, a chicken. A chicken is, so its name tells us, a bird (*tori*) in the garden (*niwa*), that is, a domesticated fowl that lives in the same space as human beings. And the opposite of the chicken/garden-bird is a bird that flies outside the garden free from human subjugation, a bird that lives in the open fields and flies when and where it wants. The garden-bird is kept cooped up, and the eggs it lays end up on the table ready for human consumption. The difference between nature outside and nature inside the garden is like this. Just as the chicken is a bird for human use, nature drawn into a garden is nature for human use. Rough, disorderly, untrammeled nature is something rather ominous. That is why the Japanese bring it into the garden and subjugate it, turn it into nature for human consumption.

Westerners do not treat nature as their own property the way the Japanese do. Like the Chinese and Koreans, for whom nature signifies preservation of the natural order, they go out to view it rather than bring it to themselves. Yet they are somewhat like the Japanese in that they see nature as something they can use to their own ends. Classical gardens of geometrial precision, like the one at Versailles, show how a human, rational order is imposed on irrational, disorderly nature. The Japanese approach to controlling nature is not to make it into something different but to leave it the way it is, only make it smaller. The rocks in a rock garden have not been carved with a chisel. And although they have been pruned, the shrubs in a Japanese garden bear no relation to the geometric shrubbery at Versailles. In short, we might say that Western-garden nature is man-made while Japanese-garden nature is made for man. The Japanese moved from waterfalls to dry landscape waterfalls. Westerners moved from waterfalls to fountains, from water flowing downward to water spurting up. The fountain represents a man-made tree; indeed, fountains are trees made of water. The water that spurts up is the tree's trunk, the water that arches out and downward forms the branches, and the spray becomes the leaves.

While the aims and methods may differ, the Japanese are very much like the Europeans in that they seek to subjugate nature and make it their own. Because the Japanese urge to control nature is so strong, they are not especially disconcerted when confronted with Western civilization and the technology it has marshaled to make use of nature. This is why the Japanese were able to assimilate it so quickly.

The Japanese are among the cleanest and tidiest of people. Their fondness for baths is well known, but there is more to it than this. For just as the samurai would never part with his sword, so the typical Japanese housewife keeps a close hold on her broom. Wiping, sweeping, washing, polishing—Japanese seem to be doing perpetual battle with dirt. Nothing comes harder to the Japanese than living with objects of no use. They cannot bear the unnecessary, the excess. As soon as they see it they sweep it up, or cut it off and throw it away. But nature without dirt is nature in a vacuum. Nature in its untrammeled state is dirty, and it has its useless elements. That is why Koreans are not so nervous about dirt. On the contrary, if a young bride is too assiduous in her dusting, if she cleans away all the dirt and makes the house altogether too spick-and-span, her old mother-in-law is apt to think it unnatural, and admonish her: "Keep that up, dear, and you'll never know good fortune. If you're too concerned about cleanliness you'll never have any children. Nothing in this world is completely without dirt. You've got to stop being so fussy and learn to take things as they are." One has to learn to accept some of the useless before one can take nature as it is and live with it.

The Japanese garden presents nature without dirt, nature tamed and trimmed and contorted. The Koreans, on the other hand, have no tradition of stunting the growth of trees. To us Koreans, the sixty varieties of pruned and stunted trees that grow along the dike of the upper garden at the Shūgaku-in Detached Palace in Kyoto display the same artificial aesthetic as is found at Versailles.

Bonsai—Delicate Chamber Music

Francis Bacon once compared colonialism to a tree. His approximate contemporary, Iemitsu (1604–51), the third Tokugawa shogun, ruler of a land which foreigners were prohibited from entering and which Japanese were strictly forbidden to leave, was planting seedling trees in tiny pots. Then he set up shelves in the flower garden of the castle, lined up his bonsai trees on them, and toyed with their well-ordered, delicate leaves. Among those bonsai trees is one that still exists and is now kept in the Imperial Palace. A five-needled pine 110 centimeters high, it is said that the shogun paid the special steward who took care of it three to five times the normal stipend. The story of how a retainer deliberately smashed one of the shogun's favorite bonsai trees because his master had become obsessed with it shows just how much Iemitsu loved bonsai.

Bonsai were not, however, unique to Japan. We know this because in the Edo period, masters of bonsai were called "camels." "Camel" was a term used for people with hunchbacks. The association with bonsai came from a reference in Chinese literature to a hunchback who had mastered the art of tree cultivation. And we know from historical records that Koreans were already cultivating bonsai pines and plum trees by the late 1460s. Yet Japan is where bonsai flourished. Westerners, who were eager to "plant a tree" in an unknown continent, were not interested in tiny box gardens. Neither were the Chinese, builders of the Great Wall; nor were the Koreans, who preferred raising orchids to their natural size. There were no professional bonsai growers in China, Korea, or the West, though there were in Japan. There are no "bonsai districts" in Korean cities as there are in some Japanese cities. There is no other bonsai association like that in Japan, which claims several million members.

Bonsai and *bonseki* (a rock or rocks arranged in a tray) are products of the same imagination that created rock gardens and tiny courtyard gardens. They are the product of a culture that puts one box inside another, and that inside still another. There is a logic in the rock garden being made even smaller and becoming the *bonseki*, just as there is in the shrubs of the veranda garden being further pruned and becoming bonsai. In the process, nature is quietly removed from the garden and placed on the ceremonial shelf indoors, there to become a kind of delicate chamber music.

First nature is pared down, simplified, and brought to the veranda in the form of a dry landscape. This in turn is further contracted, brought into the house, and put on the shelf in the form of bonsai, the *bonseki*, and tray gardens. Bringing nature closer to one means transforming it from nature that is seen to nature that is felt. The impulse to bring nature ever closer, to feel it against one's skin, led eventually to dwarfed trees small enough to fit in the palm of the hand, known as *mame* bonsai. Not content with nature next to their veranda, the Japanese yanked it in next to their pillow.

It is clear that these tray creations are reduced versions of the garden aesthetic, for the rock and sand on a *bonseki* tray are not just rock and sand; they are meant to represent a mountain and the sea. That is why in the Muromachi period (1336–1568) *bonseki*, which literally means "tray rocks," were referred to as "tray mountains." The rock or rocks in a *bonseki* are arranged and the sand raked so as to suggest some famous scenic spot, just as with a contracted scenery garden, but in the case of the *bonseki* the scenery is reproduced on a tray.

In his *Bonseki no fu (Tribute to Bonseki)*, the Zen priest and master of Chinese poetry Kokan Shiren (1278–1346) makes it clear that *bonseki* and bonsai are gardens brought indoors. As he grew older and weaker, he could no longer take care of his garden, so "I found a fist-sized rock, placed it on the garden wall, and cleaned away the dirt. . . . Then I put it in a tray of fine green celadon over the bottom of which white sand had been spread." After this he sprinkled water on it, placed it next to his seat, sat back, and enjoyed his little "garden."

As with miniature rocks, so with tiny trees. Bonsai condense hundreds of years and vast amounts of space. They symbolize the natural scenery that nurtures fully grown trees. For example, there is a style of bonsai known as *hōkitachi* (upright broom) in which the branches sweep upward from the middle of the trunk like a broom stood on end or an open folding fan. Trees of this shape exist aplenty, the zelkovas of the Musashi Plain, for instance. Then again, take Iemitsu's famous pine bonsai referred to earlier. Its twisted trunk, which looks as though it has endured countless storms, brings to mind not just a reduced copy of one tree, but a whole deluge of associations—from sea breezes to salt spray—related to the natural setting of pine trees.

Bonsai trees are shaped so as to conjure up images of natural scenes. The sight of a bonsai whose branches have been bent back upward to form a new trunk suggests a mountain tree that has been blown to the ground in a blizzard. The style of growing a number of tiny trunks from a single root calls to mind a grove of trees on a plain. Entangling a tree's roots among rocks suggests a mountain waterfall; growing a tree on a rock and placing it in water, an island in the sea. Isn't this what Tachibana no Toshitsuna was writing about in his *Sakuteiki*? He was discussing the rhetoric of rocks, that is, the way scenes are re-created in reduced form by "arranging rocks." With bonsai, the same thing is done by "arranging a tree," which is the expression used in Japanese to describe the cultivation of a bonsai tree.

The copying of nature seen in the bonsai goes beyond mere spatial considerations such as size or arrangement of branches. For example, the tiny branches of cedars and oaks which normally grow, precarious and stunted, on steep precipices are deliberately bleached—just as a natural tree's branches would be bleached with weathering and age—to give a sense that the bonsai is hundreds of years old. The bark of a bonsai tree is sometimes roughened, or holes bored into it, to complete the picture. Tachibana no Toshitsuna said that the most important technique in rock arrangement was "arranging the rocks firmly." In bonsai, the three basic elements of form are "the rising of the trunk," "the subjugation of the branches," and "the tenacity of the roots." The aesthetic of solidly planted rocks and that of roots firmly embedded in the ground conveys a downward moving power like that of a waterfall, the opposite of the Western fountain ever spurting skyward.

We see from the above that the smaller we shrink nature the more control we can have over it, and the more it bears the mark of human interference. We might say that bonsai is foot binding applied to nature; it is like binding the feet of a slave woman and making her perform a lovely dance. In order to "arrange" a bonsai tree, various tools are called for. There are clippers for clipping leaves, pruning branches, and cutting off buds. And to emphasize nature (how ironic, such "kindness"!), to make it appear more natural, wire is needed. To suppress nature's innate aspiration toward growth, to restrict natural freedom to a fixed shape, human interference is required.

Things that have been deliberately reduced and things that are simply small by nature are entirely different. Something which has been reduced is dynamic and contains the potential for change. To reduce something presupposes that it was originally relatively large and expansive. Thus even the bonsai itself can, and has been, contracted, from huge bonsai that require a crane to be lifted, to large-sized bonsai (those over ninety centimeters in height), to medium-sized bonsai (about fifty centimeters high), to the so-called "one hand" bonsai, to small bonsai (about twenty-five centimeters high), and finally to the tiny *mame* bonsai. With the *mame* bonsai, the desire to hold nature in the palm of one's hand has been realized. At their largest, *mame* bonsai are only eight centimeters high. But there are, so it is said, *mame* bonsai only a centimeter high. So small are they that they have to be examined with a magnifying glass.

Ikebana—Cosmic Flower Petals
No better entree exists to an examination of the Japanese art of flower arranging (*kadō*, or *ikebana*) than a famous episode con-

cerning the tea master Sen no Rikyū (1522–91) and his patron Toyotomi Hideyoshi. The latter had been delighted one day by the profusion of morning glories in the tea garden, so he ordered Sen no Rikyū to perform a tea ceremony. But when the time came for the ceremony and Hideyoshi made his way to the teahouse, every last one of the morning glories had been picked. Short-tempered man that he was, the general stormed furious into the tea room, there to find a single chaste morning glory in a vase on the ceremonial shelf.

Just as flowers blooming profusely in the open fields are alien to the Japanese approach to gardening, so gazing on morning glories blooming in the garden is not part of the Japanese concept of flower arranging. All the schools and styles of flower arranging in Japan share one common rule: reduce natural flowers and move them into the room.

The art of *ikebana* begins, therefore, with cutting. The contemporary master Hayakawa Shōdō, in his *Shōdō kashinshō* (*Shōdō's Selected Notes on the Spirit of Flowers*), gives a cut-and-dried summation of the principles of Japanese flower arranging:

> Plants with their roots intact are not suitable for *ikebana*. One has to start by cutting. Cut trees. Cut grasses. Cut branches. Cut leaves. Cut flowers.

Tachibana no Toshitsuna wrote of arranging rocks to "represent the sea, a great river, a mountain river, marshland, or rushes." The *Sendenshō* (*Notes on a Hermit's Teachings*), a Muromachi period text on flower arranging, takes a similar approach to flowers:

> One should try to produce scenes suggesting a marsh's edge, a river, or an inlet when one is working with flowers that normally grow near the water's edge. Field

flowers should be arranged to suggest a field, and mountain flowers to suggest mountains. Each type of flower is to be arranged in accordance with the scenery in which it naturally grows.

If gardening is the creation of a small-scale copy of nature with rocks, then flower arranging is the reproduction of nature using flowers. *Ikebana* artists would go further and declare that flower arranging is an even more idealistic reduction of the universe than gardening. As is proclaimed in the *Ikenobō Sen'ō kōden* (*The Oral Traditions of Ikenobō Sen'ō*):

What could be more exhausting and troublesome than building a mountain inside a garden, or trying to force a pond into a walled compound? With just a little water and a foot-long flower countless fine scenes of rivers and mountains can be represented; in a few brief moments, a thousand, ten thousand transformations can be wrought.

The first piece of advice one is given regarding the Japanese garden is: "Don't look at the rocks, look at the arrangement of the rocks!" Translated into the terms of flower arranging, this becomes: "Don't look at the beauty of the flowers, look at the beauty of the arrangement!" In this way, the Japanese approach is quite different from that of the West, where flowers tend to be gathered into bouquets, and different again from the Chinese and Korean approach to placing flowers in a vase. Only the Japanese use flowers to copy and reduce some larger natural scene and bring it into a smaller space.

To produce this scaled-down copy of the world, the Japanese first have to disassemble nature, a task they undertake in a manner quite their own. They tear a clump of flowers, leaves, and branches from its natural environment. Then they go at it with scissors and wire the way a factory worker would go at a bolt with a wrench. All this they do in the pursuit of a beautiful arrangement, and in this way they use flowers, leaves, and branches to create something that the gods themselves could not create.

There are seven terms often used to describe the ways in which branch placement reduces a large natural scene into a small arrangement: *in*, the passive principle of shade; *yō*, the active principle of sun; summit; peak; waterfall; a town; and the lower slopes of a mountain. Each branch in this style of flower arrangement has its place in the scheme. One branch represents a towering peak reaching toward the heavens; another, a mountain; another, a waterfall cascading hundreds of meters. A branch arranged to show horizontal rather than vertical movement becomes a cluster of little roofs, a plain, or a river. To represent a mountain and a field, flowers and branches are arranged to give a kind of perspective. As the *Sendenshō* states:

> Mountains appear in the background; fields are visible in the foreground. Flowers arranged with this spatial scheme in mind will give the feeling of a mountain in the back of the arrangement and a field in front, though the mountain should not be overemphasized.

In addition to expressing the spatial qualities of distance, flower arranging must also express the flow of time. Past and present are conveyed by the use of seasonal flowers. While the branches dictate the spatial aspects of the arrangement, the seasonal flower provides a temporal quality. Though it is beyond human capability to prevent a flower from dying—that is, to expand time—it is possible to use a flower to freeze and reduce time. This idea is explored in a section of the *Sendenshō* dealing with lotus flowers: "The flowers should be arranged so as to indicate the three ages." The "three ages" are the past, the present, and the future. The past is expressed by a lotus blossom that has lost its leaves and is about to fall apart. The present is shown by a lotus blossom in full bloom. The future is conveyed by a lotus bud and tightly rolled leaves that have yet to unfurl.

When the spatial quality of the branches and the temporal quality of the flowers are combined, the result is a representation of the universe itself. The Buddhist cosmos, dominated by Mount Sumeru, is reproduced in the garden. Ikenobō Senkō, successor to Sen'ō, sought to reproduce the ideal cosmos through the arrangement of branches and flowers. He believed this could be done by imparting an overall circular shape to the arrangement, for in the round shape of a flower the universe is reduced in the extreme.

The history of flower arrangement is the history of reductionism, and the history of scissors. In the Heian period (794–1184), people favored large groupings. For Murasaki Shikibu, author of the *Tale of Genji*, flower arrangement meant the disposition of two-meter-long cherry branches. Her contemporary and rival, Sei Shōnagon, held similar ideas, as we can see from the following passage from the *Pillow Book*: "How charming it is to break off a large branch of lovely flowering cherry and place it in a big vase." The *Rikka kōden daiji* (*Important Traditions of Rikka*), a manual written at the beginning of the seventeenth century describing the *rikka* style, says: "Arrangements in large vases can be two meters or more in height." The early *rikka* master Ikenobō Senkō perfected a style of large arrangement suitable for shelves that stretched the width of a big room. But these large arrangements gradually gave way, like bonsai, to smaller ones, and *ikebana* as we know it today was born. *Ikebana* is the opposite of the Western bouquet, which seeks to express the size of the world by the addition of ever more flowers. *Ikebana* cuts away at the flowers, the branches, the leaves, and makes empty spaces in order to capture the universe.

Let us take a look at the history of the single camellia in the

Ikenobō tradition. In *Ikebana hyakki* (*One Hundred Rules for Ikebana*), written in 1816, Ikenobō Sentei held that in arranging a single camellia only six and a half leaves are to be left on the stem. He maintained that the beauty of the camellia would emerge when the excess leaves were severely stripped away to reveal its simple, pure essence. But after Sentei came Senmyō, who carried the process to even further extremes. He cut away even more and his camellia was left with only three and a half leaves.

Sen no Rikyū denuded his master's garden of all its morning glories, and the one remaining bloom was brought into the tea room. But that one bloom had the intensity of a hundred morning glories.

The God on the Ceremonial Shelf and the Urban Recluse

In *Nihonjin no bi-ishiki* (*The Aesthetic Consciousness of the Japanese*, by Yamazaki Masakazu et al.) it is noted that the form of Japanese dance known as *mai*, usually associated with Nō and sacred shrine dances, does not include much spinning or whirling around. An integral part of Western ballet, spinning, which seems oriented heavenward as though the dancer seeks to fly away, is a common feature too of Chinese and Korean dance. Japan alone does not make use of revolving or rising movement.

What are we to make of this phenomenon? As we have already shown, the Japanese attitude toward the gods, like their attitude toward nature, involves a pulling in rather than a reaching out. The image is not one of climbing upward to meet the gods but of the gods coming down from heaven to us. It is so that the gods can descend that the Yorishiro Pine, acting as a stairway from heaven, is painted on the rear wall of a Nō stage. The Nō dancer is taught to dance in the small area inhabited by the god of the Yorishiro Pine. There is, therefore, no need for jumping in the dance, and indeed the basic posture of Japanese dance is a near crouch.

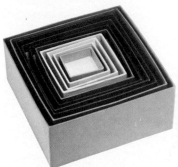

Boxes within boxes.

Box lunch.

Folding fans.

Artisan crafting miniatures.

Kokeshi dolls.

Anesama doll.
Courtesy of Isetatsu.

Hokusai's *Wave*.

Kendō fencers assuming attitude and sitting in *seiza*.

Shop curtain with crest.

Short jacket with crest.

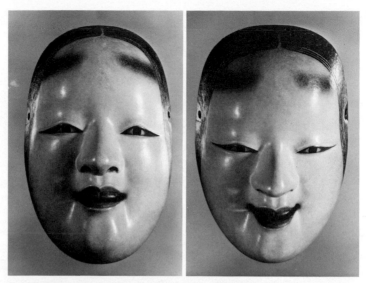

Two aspects of a Nō mask. Photo: K. Kaneko.

Ryōan Temple garden.

Portable Shinto shrine.

God shelf.

Buddhist household altar.

102

Rokusō-an teahouse. Tokyo National Museum.

Rokusō-an tea room.

Nō stage with (left) *hashigakari*. Photo: K. Kaneko.

Wafer-thin calculator (less than 1 mm in thickness).

Japanese-language word processor, combining keyboard, memory, and printer.

Hand-held radio and television.

Motor scooter with collapsible handlebars and seat (1.1 m long).

In Korean, dance is called *chum*, and some scholars have theorized that the word was derived from a verb meaning "to soar aloft." While there are many types of Korean dance, the most basic is probably the crane dance, in which the dancer represents a bird in flight. Analyzing the fundamental movements of such a dance, we see that the dancer is opening him or herself up to the world, and also symbolically seeking to transcend this world. Almost all Korean dance movement is expansive, like a wave, and involves flowing movements like those of a bird or a drifting cloud. Furthermore, the dances of priestesses in Korea feature repeated leaps.

The tree and dance as means of beckoning the gods are not, conceptually speaking, unique to Japan. In the study of mythology, the tree that joins heaven and earth is known as the "world tree," or the "cosmic tree," and it appears in nearly all primitive religions. But where the Japanese differ is in the constricting impulse that has them coaxing the gods into their very homes.

Mountains reveal a similar approach. According to the native Japanese beliefs collectively known as Shinto, "the way of the gods," when a particular mountain is considered sacred, devotees must climb to the mountain's summit, to the inner shrine, there to meet the mountain god. At least in this respect, Japanese religious practice differs little from that of other cultures. But the Japanese proceed to build a middle shrine halfway down the mountain and closer to the village at the mountain's foot. They then build a shrine in the village itself, thus pulling the mountain and its god even closer. Nor does the process end here. The god brought down from the top of the mountain has a portable shrine, so that at festival time he can be carried into the heart of the neighborhood. In this way the god can be delivered like mail to the several districts in his purview. But this is, as it were, merely an intermediary stage. The portable shrine is even further reduced, and the god pulled even closer, right into the home and onto his own shelf, the "god shelf" (*kamidana*), where he sits, reduced to intimate accessibility like the bonsai or the single arranged flower. Several gods—a paper slip representing the Sun Goddess from Ise Shrine, perhaps, alongside the tutelary god of the locality, and one of the deities thought to bring prosperity—all sit together on the shelf like tiny bonsai trees.

Buddhism, too, becomes caught up in the reduction process, as a visit to any temple will reveal. Like boxes within boxes, inside the temple there is another smaller "temple," and inside *that* temple is the image of the Buddha to be worshiped. These smaller temples within temples are called *zushi*, and they have found their way into the Japanese home, there to become the Buddhist household altar (*butsudan*). Just as the shrine was shrunk to the "god shelf," so the temple was made smaller and equipped with an image of the Buddha and the three altar utensils (an incense burner, a flower vase, and a candlestick) for use in the home.

If the shrine and the temple are the theaters of religion, the god shelf and the Buddhist household altar are its television sets. Television, after all, fulfills in its capacity to draw the world into one's home the same sort of function as the god shelf and the household altar. Indeed, the Japanese temperament is perfectly suited for television culture. The news, the scenery, the topics of the great, wide world are condensed and brought right into one's home. In many a tiny Japanese apartment the television has figuratively been placed on the ceremonial shelf. It has been suggested that the Japanese are particularly sensitive to the concept of information. The gathering and communication of information for them involves extracting what is useful among all the things that have occurred in the outside world, abbreviating it, reducing it, bringing it into the home. The main attribute of this "information" is that it is the outside brought in, and the most appropriate agent for its propagation is television. Japan's television culture illustrates perfectly the country's "folding fan" approach toward the world, an approach that seeks to bring the world indoors just as it would coax the gods into the house.

Few would dispute the contention that television occupies a highly important place in the lives of Japanese. The evidence is everywhere: in the number of channels used in Japan, in the fact that the television schedules are printed on the outside page of the morning and evening newspapers, and in the long hours of broadcasting every day. A recent survey asked people in Japan and the United States which of the following they would choose if they could only keep one: television, newspaper, telephone, automobile, or refrigerator. While a mere three percent of the Americans polled chose the television, thirty-one percent of the Japanese gave that response. In terms of viewing time, a Nielsen study conducted in 1980 showed that the typical Tokyo household averaged eight hours and twelve minutes of daily viewing compared to the American average of six hours and forty-four minutes. A UNESCO report has labeled Japan the number-one country in the world for television viewing.

The Japanese have shrunk their television world so small now that it fits onto the palm of the hand, or on the wrist in the form of a television wristwatch.

The events of the world are reduced and condensed until they fit on the television screens in people's homes. Nature too, as we have seen, is brought into the home. The flowers that were banished from the rock garden become *ikebana*, and the trees become bonsai. But what happens to the stream and pond water that the sand replaced? The answer to that is found in the tea room. The water becomes tea, and joins the flowers in the four-and-a-half-mat area (each mat, one meter by two) that comprises a typical tea room. The water has been transformed from nature that can be seen and touched to nature that can be drunk. The vast universe is forcibly squeezed into the round tea bowl, where it becomes drops of liquid that enter the human body. The relationship between seeing and being seen, between touching and being touched is extinguished, and through tea the human being and nature become one.

If rocks are nature's bones then water is its blood. When nature's blood enters the human body, the result is life. To drink tea is to bring nature, the power of the universe, into one's own body. It refreshes and cleanses one's being. It is a ritual purification of the spirit. In Zen Buddhism this is called *ichimi dōshin,* "with one taste, hearts unite." By drinking the same tea that is offered to the Buddha, one's essence unites with the Buddha and the two become one. As the Korean Zen monk Choui wrote in *Ch'asinjŏn (The Sacred Traditions of Tea),* tea is made with water that comes cascading down from soaring mountains or bubbling up through springs from deep in the earth. Thus tea embodies these natural phenomena. In short, "Tea is the god of water; water is the essence of tea."

Water itself is thin, without density. To transform it into a liquid suffused with the fragrance and deep color of green tea is similar to taking flowers from the fields and making an *ikebana* arrangement, or to growing bonsai with the trees of the mountain forests. Tea becomes the water of life, reduced for human consumption. Emperor Saga (786–842) composed the line "offering a cup of tea to the mountain spirits" before taking a drink himself. Clearly tea is no ordinary drink, for in it reside the gods of the mountains.

The reductive impulse, which sought to pull nature closer to people's daily lives, resulted in the tea room. Just pass through the side gate of an urban dwelling and there, right where you are standing, is a recluse's mountain hermitage, the sort of hut that you would expect to find only after walking deep into the hills. The path and staggered stepping-stones running from the main house are "the narrow road inland" (as Bashō called his most famous *haiku* diary), leading the visitor to a place far removed from the everyday world.

When Sen no Rikyū was asked what inspired the design of the path that led to his teahouse, he replied: "I took to heart the old poem: 'Making my way through / Fallen, yellow oak leaves /

Piled underfoot— / How desolate this path / Leading to a mountain temple!' " A teahouse, then, is a hermit's mountain hut brought to the crossroads of human activity. The Portuguese missionary Joao Rodriguez (1561–1634) was not mistaken when he wrote that the teahouse was like a country farmhouse or like the grass hut of a hermit deep in the mountains. No wonder the merchants of Sakai, where the tea ceremony as we know it today first became popular, called the teahouse "a mountain hermitage in the city" and "an urban retreat." The teahouse, which allows one to savor the life of the recluse while ensconced in the middle of the city, is a triumph of the Japanese sense of expediency and pragmatism. For Chinese and Koreans, one of the great dilemmas of life is whether to live in the city or whether to return to the countryside. The ideal is to live happily and self-sufficiently in nature. The reality is to live in the city, covered with the dust of everyday existence and caught up in the vicissitudes of human life. In Korean poetry, the dilemma is symbolized by birds. The white gull represents the hermit, gone off to live with nature. The black kite and the sparrow represent life in the everyday world.

The choice between these worlds is a conceptual one of all but insuperable difficulty. But the Japanese are not especially comfortable with concepts, or with the abstract consideration of transcendent ideals. To those who would enjoy the mountain hermit's life in an urban teahouse, there does not seem to be any point in worrying about such things. To them the Chinese poet Tao Yuanming, who resigned his office and retired from the world, would appear to be crazy. To be sure, there exists in Japan the tradition of the literary hermit. The names of Yoshishige no Yasutane (?–1002), Kamo no Chōmei (1155–1216), and Yoshida Kenkō (1283–1350) spring to mind. But unlike their Chinese and Korean counterparts, they have tended to remain outside the mainstream of their country's literature. In his book *Tsurezuregusa* (*Essays in Idleness*), Kenkō mentions a particular Chinese hermit but concludes that "there is no sense in even telling his story" to Japanese readers. This gives some indication of how weak the tradition of the hermit is in Japan.

Many of those recluses whom we do find in Japanese history differ from their Korean and Chinese counterparts in one important way. Although they claimed to have renounced the world, they maintained close ties with the most powerful men of their day. For example, the poet-priest Toren was looked after by Taira no Kiyomori (1118–81), who was the virtual ruler of Japan in the last years of his life. Kenkō, too, was close to those in power. For the Japanese it was not a question of choosing one or the other, of living in the world or retiring completely from it, for they cleverly devised a way to do both at the same time. The Japanese hermit savors the politics of the world, even from his retreat. The worldly man can enjoy the flavor of a mountain village even in the city. In the midst of his prosperity and power he can have a taste of poverty. Though married, he can sample the religious life just like a monk.

In a society where principle is not treated as important and where there is no ideology, expediency cannot help but become the standard by which actions are judged. Certainly it is more expedient, and more pleasurable, to act out a hermit's existence in an urban teahouse than to renounce the world and go out and actually live in the mountains. If anything, this playacting is actually more interesting, dramatic, and moving than real life. In the same way, a bonsai seems more natural than a real tree, and the shore represented by an arrangement of rocks in a garden is more beautiful than the sea itself.

Thus is concept transformed in Japan by emotions, images, and art. Japan was able to modernize so quickly, to assimilate Western ideas so easily, because its people have never adhered to the Chinese and Korean concept of nature as a force standing in opposition to a materialistic approach to the world.

REDUCTIONISM AS FOUND IN PEOPLE AND SOCIETY

Understanding the Four-and-a-half-mat Space

What kind of house do the Japanese live in, these people who have shrunk mountains, rivers, trees, even the gods and Buddhas, and placed them on the shelf? A place very foreign to the experience of other peoples, if one considers that *tatami* mats, the ceremonial shelf, the tea room have no equivalents in Europe, China, or Korea. With the exception of the great mansions of the feudal lords, some of which covered thirty or more hectares, the Japanese house is essentially a small, densely packed place. In the nineteenth century Europeans chose such phrases as "paper houses" and "matchbox houses" to describe them. A century later, the infamous "rabbit hutch" made its appearance. To be sure, a rabbit hutch is more solid than a paper house and larger than a matchbox, but the characterization came as an enormous shock to the Japanese because it was so obviously negative. The problem was that the "rabbit hutch" charge did not appear in some nineteenth century European's impressionistic travel diary or in a poem or novel. No, it was leaked from a secret Common Market report compiled in 1979 and was all the more stinging for that. What made it even worse was that it came coupled with the word "workaholic," used as an epithet for the Japanese.

Emotive terms aside, there are certain realities that affect the state of housing in Japan. On the average it costs at least six times the average annual income of a white-collar worker to buy a house in Japan. This is appreciably higher than in Europe or

America. Combine this with land costs that are about five times what they are in the rest of the world and the inevitable result is small houses on very expensive plots of land.

But what do the Japanese themselves think about this situation? Perhaps if they could step outside of themselves they might say this to their "rabbit hutch" critics: You must understand that it is not so much that we put up with small dwellings for lack of anything else as that we have long actually preferred to live in narrower confines. For us the three qualities of an ideal house are that it be conveniently located, big, and cheap. Yes, "big"— but you have to remember that our traditional attitude toward living space is quite different from that prevalent in the West. Did you know that people would often build a four-and-a-half-mat (six-square-meter) hut in their garden and actually spend more time in it than in the main house—and enjoy it more? You are probably unfamiliar with the Japanese word *kojinmari* (snug) or the proverb "small house, big heart." You probably never stopped to think we might enjoy a small space precisely because it is small. Have you ever ridden on a Japanese train when it is not crowded? If you have, you will have seen that even though there are plenty of empty seats, people huddle together in one small area, not so much like rabbits as like cats dozing peacefully.

Perhaps sceptical Westerners will need another example. During the Meiji era, when Western-style buildings were in vogue, the Marquis Maeda constructed a fine Western-style villa of some 2,500 square meters at the cost of about $2.5 million in today's money. But he only put up guests there. He himself preferred to live in a small, old-fashioned, Japanese-style "paper house." For further substantiation, let us take a rather more academic tack and consult that classic of medieval literature, Kamo no Chō-mei's *Hōjōki* (*An Account of My Hut*). "Our dwellings are fleeting . . . like dew on a morning glory," he says of his attitude toward houses. And he goes on:

Look at the fish and birds. A fish never tires of water, yet if one is not a fish one cannot understand its feelings. Birds long for the forest, yet not being birds we do not know why. The pleasures of solitary life in my small hut are no different. Unless one has lived this way, one cannot understand it.

Chōmei's "small hut" was four-and-a-half mats large, less than one-third the size of a small apartment in Tokyo today.

The Japanese attitude toward living space is based on something unique to Japan: the woven straw mat, *tatami*, which measures two meters by one. The old proverb "Half a mat when you're up, one mat when you're asleep" sums it all up. One two-by-one-meter mat is all you need.

But *tatami* mats are more than just something spread on the floor. Since the sixteenth century they have dictated the size of houses; they are the standard by which to measure the width between pillars. Because the *tatami* mat dictated the size of the room, not the other way around, it was used as a unit for determining taxes in Kyoto. Tax evasion being a universal human activity, *tatami* mats have always been slightly larger in Kyoto than elsewhere in Japan.

In the Heian period (794–1184), *tatami* mats did not cover the whole of the floor but were only placed in determined parts of the room. The size of a mat depended on court rank, a 1.3-by-2-meter mat for people of the first rank, 1.3 by 1.6 for people of the second rank, and so on.

It was in the Muromachi period (1336–1568) that *tatami* mats came to cover the whole of the floor. This was just when such arts as Nō drama, tea ceremony, flower arranging, and gardening were beginning to give the nation's culture a distinctively Japanese hue. So much of what we consider unique to Japanese culture, so many of those of its manifestations that cannot be found on the Asian continent, seem to be closely related to the four-and-a-half-mat room.

Look at ancient Greece. Its culture revolved around the *agora*, the town plaza. Morning was "the time when the *agora* fills up." Afternoon was "the time when the *agora* empties." Greek art, rhetoric, philosophy, politics—all was centered on the *agora*. And what could be a more fitting art form for a broad expanse than large-scale sculpture, which makes use of light and shade? On the other hand, try to picture a flower arrangement taken from its shelf in the Japanese tea room and placed among the soaring columns of the Acropolis. Or try to imagine a group of Athenians quietly composing linked poetry in the middle of the *agora*. A flower arrangement or a bonsai tree would not survive for long in that environment, for these are arts that developed with the advent of the tiny straw mat. A rock garden would be out of place there too; it is designed to be viewed from and embraced by the four-and-a-half-mat room.

Heirs to the Greek tradition of the *agora*, Westerners find stability in wide-open spaces. Japanese, on the other hand, are more comfortable on the four-and-a-half mats of the tea room. Many are gripped with agoraphobia when they find themselves in a wide, open area. They feel ill at ease and unsure of what to do, as any number of examples demonstrate. The story goes, for instance, that when Japan's representative to the Washington Disarmament Conference of 1921, Katō Tomosaburō, was faced with a totally unexpected proposal from the American delegation at the very opening of the conference, he rushed back to his hotel and locked himself in the bathroom to cool down and decide what to do next.

Many Japanese cannot relax unless they are in a confined area. Should we be surprised, then, that Japan has come up with the "capsule hotel," where the "rooms" are not much bigger than a refrigerator placed on its side? In Tokyo alone there were, as of late 1981, five of these hotels with a total of about a thousand "rooms," and the number is expected to increase at least ten times in the next few years. Each capsule room is about the size of one *tatami* mat, but everything one needs is built in: television, radio, digital alarm clock, and phone connected to the front desk. It was reported recently in the Japanese edition of *Playboy* magazine (6 October 1981) that a "capsule subculture" has developed, that people actually rent these tiny spaces in order to meditate, practice the guitar, or just read!

Different attitudes toward space in Japan and the West are also evident in the approach to disciplining children. When confronted with a misbehaving child, the Western parent might shut it up in a small place, or at least threaten to do so: "If you don't do what I say I'm going to lock you in the closet." Japanese children, on the other hand, often regard a closet as a refuge, and it is not unusual for a child to hide in the closet and fall fast asleep. Thinking that the child has gone out to play, the parents start to worry. Eventually a frantic search is launched, and all the while the child is blissfully sleeping in the closet.

The Japanese four-and-a-half-mat room provides the perfect stage for the intimate appreciation of Japanese art. This is not just because of its association with the tea ceremony, for the four-and-a-half-mat standard predates the tea ritual in Japan. The word used for the abbot's room in a Zen temple (*hōjō*) originally meant "four-and-a-half mats," and the garden outside that room was called the "four-and-a-half-mat garden" (*hōjōtei*), even if it was not always that small. The four-and-a-half-mat room, then, was Japan's sacred enclosure, nurturing the rock garden, Japanese Buddhism, and above all the tea ceremony and its related arts.

In simplifying and paring down room decoration and reducing the size of the room itself, the Japanese discovered their New World—the tea ceremony. It is interesting to note that Columbus sailed across the ocean on his way to the New World at about the same time that Murata Jukō discovered his New World by sectioning off a four-and-a-half-mat portion of his study.

Tea was not always associated in Japan with a small room. Tea-tasting competitions were introduced from China in the fourteenth century, and they were held in two-story tea shops. Somewhat later, the painter and poet Nōami (1397–1471) began to hold more formal tea parties in his home. Both these types of gatherings were sumptuous, large-scale affairs, not all that far removed from their Chinese antecedents. Murata Jukō, however, perceived that the spirit could not really be at ease in large rooms. His solution was to mark off a reduced area, an enclosure, and bring the tea ceremony into it, which is why the word "enclosure" is often used as a synonym for tea room.

The first four-and-a-half-mat tea room in Japan, called the Dōjinsai, was built by Jukō at Ginkaku Temple, the retirement villa of the shogun Yoshimasa (1435–90). The size was thus established as standard, and a later tea master, Takeno Jōō (1502–1555), set about simplifying the decoration of the tea room by leaving the earthen walls unpapered and the wood trim unvarnished. So influential was his style that the terms "tea room," "four-and-a-half mats," and "Jōō" became synonymous. The reductive aesthetics of *ikebana*, where leaves, branches, and buds are stripped away one by one, and of the rock garden, which dispenses with trees and water, were also applied to the home, and the result was the tea ceremony as we know it today.

Sen no Rikyū brought the "grass hut" tea room to its own rough version of perfection. He sought to make it even smaller, experimenting with three-mat, two-mat, and even one-and-a-half-mat arrangements. He was not content, however, with trying to make the tea room ever smaller; he also came up with the idea of shrinking the doorway, thus creating the "crawling-in entrance" (*nijiriguchi*), so called because one could only pass through it by crawling on one's hands and knees. He is supposed to have got the idea for this seventy-centimeter-square doorway when he noticed the hatchways on the boats that plied the Yodo river.

The "crawling-in entrance" had several interesting consequences. For one thing, weapons were effectively excluded from the tea room because a warrior could not possibly manage to get through the door while wearing his swords. It was, in addition, a great equalizer, even those of the highest class having to stoop to go through it. This contracted entrance lies at the heart of the four essential components of tea ceremony: harmony, respect, purity, and elegant simplicity. At the entrance to Dante's Inferno is written, "Abandon all hope, ye who enter." Perhaps the "crawling-in entrance" to the tea room should read, "Abandon all pride, ye who enter."

The Japanese warriors squeezing through the "crawling-in entrance" and the Roman legions marching through the Arch of Constantine were worlds apart. To say that "all roads lead to Rome" is to say that the gates of Rome were open outward toward the world. Such was not the case with the "crawling-in entrance," which faced inward. Just as the gates of Rome were a symbol for expansion, so the "crawling-in entrance" stands for contraction. Even Toyotomi Hideyoshi, who once ordered Rikyū to make the entrance to his tea room larger, in the end could not help but conform to the confines of the tea room.

Hideyoshi was a rare example of an expansive personality in the midst of Japan's reduction culture. Unable to confine himself in an island country, he went so far as to launch an invasion of the Asian mainland, bringing the flames of war to the Korean peninsula. Yet even at that time, the teahouse he erected at his Kyushu encampment is said to have been only two mats in size. Contemporary records show that he covered the floor of the tiny room with a brocade carpet and took his meals there. If the writers of the Common Market report had known of Hideyoshi, they might well have expressed surprise that someone could live in a "rabbit hutch" and make war at the same time. Westerners, or even Westernized Japanese, who do not understand the pleasures of living in a small space are likely to be confused by the apparent contradictions a man like Hideyoshi presents.

Yet even among Westerners there have been those who recognized that the tea room was the ultimate expression of Japan's reduction culture. When the well-known Charles and Anne Lindbergh, expansionists both, flew to Japan over the polar route, Anne Lindbergh recorded her impressions of the tea room in eloquent terms in her diary:

> I looked with wonder at the Japanese appreciation of all small things in nature. . . . This appreciative vision, which saw beauty in the smallest things and made beauty in the most trivial acts . . . seemed to me to find its most vivid expression in the Tea Ceremony. [From Anne Morrow Lindbergh, *North to the Orient*, New York: Harcourt and Brace, 1935.]

The Tension Culture

According to legend, tea is made from the eyelids of Daruma (Bodhidharma, the legendary founder of Zen). The story goes that because his eyelids grew heavy with drowsiness while he was meditating, Daruma plucked them off and threw them into the garden where they sprouted into tea bushes. A truth resides in this tale: tea allows us to concentrate and see things with Daruma's clarity. Tea is a drink that keeps us awake. It opens our eyes, as it were, to the world around us. There is more to it than simply prosaic caffeine, as the tea ceremony shows. Because it requires the human consciousness to concentrate, the tea ceremony generates a spiritual tension and clarity that surpasses any chemical effects caffeine might have.

Standing at the opposite pole from tea is the Chinese poet Li Bo's favorite drink—wine. Li Bo's eyelids were heavy with wine as he gazed at the moon, for wine does not wake us up, it entices us into the world of sleep. Its intoxicating power is like that of gentle waves; it lulls the human mind with gentle rocking and carries it off to places far and near.

These two liquids, both of human manufacture, symbolize two different outlooks on culture.

Tea and wine have been rivals since ancient times. Their relative merits were debated in a work of the Tang dynasty (618–907) called the *Chajiulun* (*A Discussion of Tea and Wine*), and in the sixteenth century, the Japanese Buddhist priest Ranjuku wrote a similar treatise. It takes the form of an imaginary debate between Lord Bōyō (literally, "forgetting cares"), who extols the virtue of wine as something that dispels gloom in the world, and Master Dekihan (literally, "rinsing away troubles"), who maintains that anyone who does not like tea fails to understand the true Way and is not really human. The argument ends in a draw when a gentleman of leisure steps in to mediate and declares that, after all, "tea is tea and wine is wine."

The debate between tea and wine is eternal. Several hundred years before Ranjuku's treatise, the priest Eisai (1141–1215) wrote Japan's first book of tea, the *Kissa yōjōkei* (*Drinking Tea for Health*). It is said that the shogun Sanetomo (1192–1219) requested the book because he was trying to give up alcohol and was looking to tea as a healthier alternative. Tea pulls the spirit together, while wine loosens and relaxes it. In *Muchū mondō* (*Dialogues in a Dream*), the Zen priest and garden designer Musō Soseki (1275–1351) wrote that tea "dispels the darkness and opens our eyes, aiding us in our journey [toward enlightenment]." Wine, on the other hand, he called "the great inebriator" which enticed the poets into fantasy worlds. Or, to translate it into the terms of my thesis, tea is conducive to a reductive outlook, wine, to an expansive one. The Japanese have a great fondness for wine; it is the drink of their native religion. But its position in the nation's culture has to a considerable extent been usurped by tea, the reductive drink.

Tea, like so many other things, was originally imported from China and Korea. Historical records show that the use of tea by Buddhist monks in Korea long predates its appearance in Japan, although only vestiges of the practice remain in Korea today. Early Japanese records state that tea was first brought to Japan from China in the eighth century, during the Tang dynasty, by monks returning from periods of study on the continent. But neither the Chinese nor the Koreans could ever have envisioned that tea drinking in Japan would be turned into an art and a religious ritual.

In Japanese tea ceremony, drinking tea remains the purpose, but the place, utensils, and actions of the drinking are carefully prescribed. Chinese and Korean treatises on tea discuss in great detail types of tea, how to brew it, and what water to use, but they do not touch on the etiquette of drinking or the utensils to be used. It seems sometimes that for the Japanese, the tea room, the etiquette, indeed all the prescriptive particulars, are more important than the tea itself. When Hideyoshi held a huge tea gathering at the Kitano Shrine, admission was open to all, regardless of social position, and Hideyoshi proclaimed, "Those who do not have green tea may bring roasted barley instead." A tea ceremony, in other words, without tea. But is this really so strange? When you think about it, the stimulative effect of the tea ceremony results as much from the surroundings and the implicit tension in the actions as it does from the tea itself. A closer look reveals that all this is a product of the reduction outlook.

To leave the everyday world and enter the tea room is to enter into a special enclosure. In fact, the garden path leading to the tea house is likened to the "narrow white path that leads from the burning house that is this world," as described in the Buddhist sutras. The religious metaphor does not end here. Before entering the tea room the guest must rinse his mouth at the stone basin (tsukubai, which literally means "crouching") just as he would before going into a shrine or temple. The tea room, therefore, is a sacred place, apart from the mundane world. Yet there is no image of a Buddha or god to be found there, only something to drink. We cannot really say therefore that the spiritual feeling of tea and the temporary renunciation of the world that is part of the ceremony actually spring from specific religious principles. Tea has no sacred scriptures. It is not a religion, it is a performance, an art.

Dividing the outer garden from the inner garden is a gate that reminds one of the "narrow gate" of the Bible, though in a practical, not symbolic, sense. Let us take a look at how one goes about entering this "narrow gate" and taking part in the tea ceremony. If you know proper etiquette you will arrive twenty to thirty minutes before the appointed time, for all who would pass through the narrow gate must learn to wait. Until everyone has arrived, the guests remain gathered at the waiting area, looking much like a flock of sparrows.

Once all have assembled, you descend to the outer garden where you wait again at the *machiai*, a more formal, roofed waiting area. Presently the host opens the low and narrow gate and the guests stoop to pass under it one by one after bowing silently. At this point you slip into special sandals of woven bamboo to traverse the staggered stepping-stones. These stones are scattered like notes on a music sheet and produce a lovely balletic step in those who walk on them. Yet they are also strict taskmasters, forcing the human pace and rhythm to follow their layout. Large or small, male or female, the guests are united in a standard stepping pattern. In the outside world not even the lowliest servant has his pace or the direction of his step regulated so severely. Only the guests at a tea ceremony must conform in this way. These stones, which get smaller as one approaches the tea room, prepare the guest for the fact that, unlike in the outside world, every word, every action in that room is reduced to a single standard form. Finally, just before entering the tea room, you crouch at the *tsukubai* to wash your hands. With each movement you have taken on the way to the tea room, your body and actions have become progressively smaller, more contracted.

Now you must crouch again, this time on the "shoe-removing

stone" (*kutsunugi-ishi*), and then slide open the door to the tea room. But to go through that door you have to contract your body even more, for this is the "crawling-in entrance" we discussed earlier. Here is the ultimate "narrow gate."

You might think all that contracting of body and movement is now finished. But no, it has just begun! The guests all sit formally on their heels—a posture called *seiza*—and in an order dictated by status. Now the actual tea ceremony can commence. All that has gone before—the gathering together, the stooping, the crouching, the crawling—has been merely a warm-up for the ordeal of having to sit formally on your heels in the *seiza* manner.

There is a story that the potter Bernard Leach, assisting at a tea ceremony once, could not bear the pain of sitting on his heels any longer so he begged his host's forgiveness, leaned back against a pillar, and stretched out his legs. In so doing, however, he denied himself the possibility of appreciating the tea ceremony.

Leach is certainly not the only person to have found sitting *seiza* too much for him. Many foreigners have problems maintaining that posture. Animals do not consciously hold a posture; humans, however, do so as a way of giving physical expression to some spiritual or psychological aspect of culture. Westerners have always used chairs. They have never, therefore, developed a posture for sitting on the floor. While the chair is no stranger to Asia, Asians, unlike Westerners, have, over the centuries, developed a posture for sitting on the ground, and this is something that distinguishes East from West.

Look at images of the Buddha Shakyamuni. He sits with legs intertwined in the Lotus position, elbows rounded out and hands resting on his lap. It is a posture that represents the essence of Buddhism. In the West, the two postures of cultural significance have been sitting on chairs and standing. India, China, Korea, and Japan—all countries where Buddhism had a profound impact—developed postures for sitting on the ground. However, while the Japanese *seiza* posture is a form of sitting on the ground, it is far different from sitting cross-legged or in the lotus position. If anything, it differs from normal sitting postures even more than standing does, for it is a product of the tea ceremony, a ritual not to be found elsewhere in Asia. The contracted world of the four-and-a-half-mat tea room required a suitable sitting posture, and it found that posture in *seiza*.

When a lot of people are gathered in the tiny tea room, it is impossible for them all to sit in the more relaxed cross-legged position. *Seiza* was developed as a sitting posture that would save space. In normal, everyday surroundings, the Japanese are like the Koreans: men sit cross-legged and women sit with one knee brought up to the chest. But it is not enough just to think of *seiza* as an efficient way of saving space in a small area. Most elements of human culture did indeed originate as practical responses to particular situations, but they only remain as part of a culture so long as they fill some spiritual need. If *seiza* were merely a practical expedient for the tea ceremony, we would never find it outside the tea room. But in fact, as its name, which literally means "correct sitting," implies, it is the proper posture for sitting formally on the floor in Japan at any time and in any place.

If sitting cross-legged represents a relaxed, expansive mood, then sitting *seiza* shows a tight, reductive one. It pulls together body and spirit and stimulates them just like the caffeine in green tea. Dōgen gives a description of the proper meditation posture, a description that applies just as well to *seiza*:

> You should lean neither to the left nor to the right, neither forward nor backward. You must align your ears with your shoulders and your nose with your navel. Your tongue should be touching the roof of your mouth, teeth and lips pressed gently together. Keep your eyes open and breathe faintly through your nose.

Seiza is a motionless posture. Animals move easily and rest languidly. Plants rustle in the wind, clouds scuttle by, and water flows along. Everything around us is in motion. Koreans, who seek to live in harmony with this nature in flux, are not used to motionlessness. It has too much of a military aura to it. The prewar Japanese *Infantry Drill Manual* states: "Motionlessness is the soldier's basic posture. Therefore the soldier must remain outwardly unperturbed though inwardly his spirit be overflowing." Although there has been war in Korea an average of once every ten years throughout the country's history, the standard posture of Koreans has always been relaxed rather than tense and motionless. One of the most frequently used words in the Korean language translates as "to unravel" or "loosen up." It is used in a variety of situations, such as when things have reached an impasse, when troubles are mounting, or when the squeeze is on. It stands for the opposite of motionlessness since it represents the loosening of tension.

When Koreans are about to begin work they say, "Time to loosen up now." Koreans cannot imagine telling somebody who is about to begin something to "give it your all" or "take care." For them it is "Free your mind!" Whenever Koreans use a phrase like "Take care," it is not as a greeting or an encouragement; it is as a scolding or criticism. Yet in Japan you can sometimes see high-school baseball teams lined up sitting *seiza* on the ground in front of the bench. The tension this generates is exactly what relaxes the players!

Japanese often use the expression "I feel a little rusty," which is a way of comparing the human body and mind to a sword. If you fail to use a sword and to polish it frequently, it will soon get rusty. It requires constant attention—tension—in order to stay shiny and ready for effective use. The tea room provides a way to keep the rust off.

Far from seeing the body as a sword, Koreans (and Chinese too, for that matter) tend to think of it in terms of a zither. Zither strings must be left slack when not in use or they will break. The only time you tighten them up is when you are actually going to play. Koreans are brought up, not constantly polishing the sword and keeping it free of rust, but staying loose lest their "strings" break from too much tension. The unique sitting posture of the Korean literati was one in which the seated person swayed gently and rhythmically from side to side like a willow in the breeze, or a pendulum. To a Korean, sitting *seiza* is nothing less than punishment; to a Japanese it is a way of concentrating one's attention and thereby relaxing.

So different are the outlooks of the two peoples that when Korean emissaries visited Japan in the midst of the latter's civil warfare during the sixteenth century and were told that the tea room provided a place for the beleagured samurai to rest, they could not believe it. The exquisitely refined tea room appeared little more than a cave to them, and the activity that went on inside—the psychological tension generated by sitting *seiza* and following carefully prescribed rules just to drink a cup of tea— seemed hardly conducive to relaxation. But how could they have been expected to understand? Japan's peculiar tension culture, where play was work and rest was a psychological struggle for self-mastery, was completely alien to them. This is why they were convinced that Japanese tea rooms were really used as war operation centers or as hideouts.

The syntax of the tea ceremony is, as we noted earlier: gather together, stoop, crouch, crawl through, sit *seiza*. The entrance garden and tea room were designed specifically to aid in this progressive contraction of the human body. The Zen priest Myōe (1173–1232), who learned about tea from Eisai, said that drowsiness, worldly thoughts, and improper seating posture were the three poisons that obstructed Zen meditation. Tea ceremony is none other than an attempt to exorcise these three poisons.

The tea ceremony, because it stimulates the spirit by generating a positive tension, renews the mind and body and prepares one to take on a new challenge. The Japanese feel a need for an internal psychological battery that can be recharged periodically, as at the tea ceremony. That is why in Japan there are so many "Associations for the Encouragement of Something-or-other."

Another way the Japanese recharge their batteries is by binding parts of their body: tying a *hachimaki* (headband) around the head, binding up the sleeves with a cord called a *tasuki*, and girding the loins with a cloth called a *fundoshi*. By doing this a Japanese feels he has pulled his body together, concentrated his strength, and relaxed his spirit. It is significant, therefore, that warriors used the verb "contract" to describe the action of putting on their helmet before battle.

The degree to which this sense of contraction for the sake of action is important in Japan was demonstrated in a newspaper account of a *sumō* wrestling bout in the autumn tournament of 1981. Kotokaze was fighting Asashio, and on the outcome of the match hinged the question of which of the two would be promoted to the rank of *ōzeki* (champion). Asashio lost, because, it was said, his "spiritual concentration was inadequate." Kotokaze's victory was attributed to his success in concentrating his spirit down to "the point of a spear."

During the Lockheed payoff trial, Enomoto Mie was called to testify regarding the activities of her ex-husband. There was a great deal of controversy surrounding her testimony because it incriminated her former husband in the scandal, and many criticized her for lack of loyalty. Yet most were impressed by her manner on the witness stand: back straight, fiercely attentive, direct in her statements. This was more important than any social or ethical questions. It suggests an attitude of resolve that is summed up in the old proverb: "A bee stings once, then dies."

One Meeting in a Lifetime

The tea ceremony presents us with two contractions: one, we have examined, of space; the other, of time. Time, particularly as highlighted in single moments, is indispensible to tea. The *Yamanoue Sōji ki*, the seminal work on the tea ceremony by Yamanoue Sōji, a disciple of Sen no Rikyū, puts it this way:

> Even in an ordinary tea ceremony, from the time one passes through the outer gate until the time one leaves, one should treat the host with the utmost respect as if this were the only ceremony of one's lifetime.

The tea master and statesman Ii Naosuke (1815–60) expatiated on this in his book *Chanoyu ichie-shū (The One Gathering for Tea)*:

> The interaction that occurs at a tea ceremony has been described as "one meeting in a lifetime." What does this mean? Let me explain: even though host and guests may have had tea together many times before and probably will in the future as well, if they treat the ceremony at hand as the only one they will ever have, then it will in fact become a once-in-a-lifetime encounter. The host should strive as he has never done before to make everything perfect, leaving nothing inadequately attended to. He should treat the guests as though he will probably never have a chance to meet them again, and overlook nothing in his solicitude toward them. All should interact with sincerity. This is what is meant by "one meeting in a lifetime." Neither host nor guest will waste a single moment. This is what I call "the one gathering for tea."

In other countries drinking tea is regarded as a pleasurable activity. However, if it is treated as a once-in-a-lifetime event, clearly it is no ordinary tea party but serious business. Nothing the participants do, even the interaction between host and guest, can be left to chance. To achieve the ideal "one meeting in a lifetime" tea ceremony, the concentration must be as sharp as a sword.

Hovering over the "one meeting in a lifetime" concept is the specter of death. In *The Idiot*, Dostoevsky describes the last five minutes of life before the death sentence is carried out. You realize, when reading the passage, that when you are confronted with death, everything—the litter on the roadside, the glint of sunshine on a weathered roof, even the air around you—sinks into the very core of your being. Through Dostoevsky you are given "one meeting in a . lifetime" with Russia itself. A similar phenomenon occurs in your perceptions of people, of someone you love perhaps, just before death. You become acutely conscious of that person. Faced with the realization that you will never see that person again, every word, every glance, every movement takes on added significance.

To say, therefore, that a particular tea ceremony is a once-in-a-lifetime encounter is to bring death into the tea room. A meeting that can never occur again, a moment that can never be recaptured—confronted with this vision, the host and guests cannot help but "interact with sincerity." This, too, is why the tea ceremony must accord with the season and even the time of day.

The transcience of life lingers in the silent tea garden. It is the feeling expressed by Shōō when he said: "Of all the year, mid November is loneliness itself." It is what Teika wrote about in his poem:

> Gazing out and beyond
> I see no spring flowers,
> No scarlet maple leaves,
> Just one thatched hut on the beach
> In autumn's fading evening light.

When Japan's reduction mentality is expressed in temporal terms, it becomes "one meeting in a lifetime"—the essence of death distilled. This is true not only of the spirit of tea but of the spirit of flower arranging too, and indeed of the spirit of Japanese art itself.

Nowhere is this heightened perception of transcience more evident than in the attraction falling petals hold for the Japanese. This is why cherry blossoms are so special in Japan: they bloom, fade, and scatter so quickly. If flowers did not wither and die, people would not be so attached to them and would not gaze at them with the same sense of tense anticipation.

The Nō master Konparu Zenpō (1454–1532), who lived during some of the worst of Japan's civil wars, claimed that Nō had a great deal in common with the way of the warrior, and by this he meant the way of the sword and death. He wrote in his *Zenpō sarugakudan* (*Talks on Nō*): "Every day, every night, again and again, the warrior continually faces death. This is what makes him free." Since the warrior faces death constantly, his spirit is ever alert, and he lives each moment to the full. By saying that Nō is like this, Zenpō is comparing the stage to a battleground where each step, each gesture, is born of the same single-minded concentration that is possessed by the warrior facing death. To let up even a little is to invite disaster, so the actor rallies all his strength and concentration to create a life-or-death art.

Zenpō's thoughts about Nō actors and warriors are echoed by an anecdote in the *Kasshi yawa* (*Nocturnal Conversations on the First Night of a New Age*—a collection of essays by Matsuura Kiyoshi published in 1821) concerning a meeting between the master swordsman Yagyū Munenori and the head of the Kanze Nō school. The shogun Tokugawa Iemitsu (1604–51) brought Munenori along to a Nō performance and told him to watch the Nō master carefully to see if he let down his guard during the performance. After the play the shogun asked Munenori for his judgement, which the latter duly gave: "He did not let down his guard at all. But I did detect the briefest of lapses in the final dance. If I had attacked him with a sword at that instant, I think he would probably have been killed." For his part, the Nō master, once backstage, asked an associate who the man was who had been watching him so intently throughout the play. On hearing that it was the master swordsman Munenori, the actor said with satisfaction: "That explains it! I thought it was suspicious that he should watch my every move so carefully, then chuckle when I faltered at that one passage in the final dance. So that's who he is, a master swordsman."

Like sitting *seiza*, the concept of "one meeting in a lifetime" generates the kind of tension essential to Japanese culture. The temporal reduction implicit in this idea is reflected in the expression *isshōkenmei* (as hard as one can; for all one is worth), which originally meant "to guard a place with one's life" but has now come to mean going at something wholeheartedly and enthusiastically. The expression, which has no obvious equivalent in China or Korea, indicates the way Japanese go about any undertaking—intensely, as if each moment were life's last—and helps to explain why they have been so successful at making and exporting everything from transistors to cameras to cars. Clearly, to live for all one is worth is to live with the constant specter of death, making each moment as full as possible.

A strange shadow lingers over everything in Japan, from sex, to the marketplace, to the tea room: the shadow of death. While most of us turn away from death, the Japanese embrace it, draw it closer, and try to make use of its fearsome power.

The *Encyclopaedia Britannica* characterizes suicide in Japan as: "the violent ending of one's own life by drowning oneself, jumping off a cliff, hanging oneself, taking poison, stabbing oneself with a sword, and so on." The West has long believed that Japan views suicide this way. Even now, one of the first images that Japan evokes among Westerners is precisely this, ritual disembowelment (*harakiri*, or more properly, *seppuku*). Westerners imagine that death is treated by the Japanese as a matter of no great consequence. But it is not because they take death lightly that the Japanese are preoccupied with it. Rather, it is just the opposite. It is because they fear death and seek to avoid it that they embrace it so.

I was in the United States in 1970 when the Japanese novelist Yukio Mishima killed himself by ritual disembowelment. It had caused quite a stir there; even taxi drivers were talking about it. It was not so much that Mishima had a lot of fans in the United States as that people wondered how a well-known writer from an advanced nation like Japan could have committed suicide in such an old-fashioned way. They could not understand how one culture could encompass both sophisticated electronics that dominated world markets and a novelist who committed *seppuku* with a samurai sword.

I noticed with some bitterness that the newspapers, rather than devoting their attention to Mishima's literary accomplishments, turned out articles like "What is *harakiri*?" I myself was asked more than once by people to explain what it meant. Ignoring the fact that I am Korean, I did my best to explain. *Seppuku*, I pointed out, is a ritual, a death ritual, and a ritual by definition is different from the mundane actions we perform every day. The tea ceremony too is a ritual for the Japanese, one that they have been practicing for centuries. Even if the tea ceremony is held daily, it is always performed as though it were a once-in-a-lifetime event. In that sense, the ritual of tea and the ritual of death are related. Whether they left any the wiser about *seppuku* I do not know.

As should be clear by now, Japanese tea ceremony is not simply a matter of drinking tea, of taking in tannic acid and caffeine. The tea ceremony grew out of tea gatherings, and the concept of "gathering together" (*yoriai*) is as important to the tea ceremony as caffeine is to tea. In fact, the Kamakura and Muromachi forerunners of the tea ceremony were called simply "gatherings" or "tea gatherings." *Yoriai*, according to the dictionaries, means "to press in closer" or "to come or bring together in one place."

Applied to the tea ceremony, therefore, it means reducing the distance between people and packing them into one area, that is, the tea room.

In fact, like the tea ceremony itself, the idea of "gathering together" is a key component of Japan's reduction culture. We have already discussed how in Japan, nature and even the gods are drawn toward humans through such activities as gardening, flower arranging, the portable shrine, and so on. Gathering together represents the same kind of action applied to the tea room. Although the tea room consists of four-and-a-half mats, the guests themselves really only have an area of two mats, two meters by two, to sit on (or even less in some of Rikyū's tea rooms). Thus, even if the guests are mutual enemies they are forced to press in close together, to the point where they are actually touching. The concepts of "gathering together" and "touching" combined to narrow the boundaries of the tea room.

Touching in Japanese has many shades of meaning. For example, "to allow a person one's skin" (*hada o yurusu*) means to trust that person, and "to take off a layer of skin" (*hitohada nugu*) for someone is to do everything one can to help him or her. "Congenial to one's skin" (*hada ga au*) might sound a bit erotic, but in Japanese it simply means that something suits one. That is why a newspaper account of the meeting in Ottawa between the then prime minister of Japan, Suzuki Zenkō, and U.S. President Ronald Reagan began with the subheading "They found each other's skin congenial."

In Japan what binds people together is not the mind or the heart, it is a more concrete and experiential tactile contact. The nationalist scholar Motoori Norinaga (1730–1801), who might perhaps be called the father of interpreters of Japan, implicitly recognized this when he wrote that whereas Chinese culture was based on a sense of morality, Japanese culture was based on a sense of beauty and sentiment. His theory applies equally well to human relationships: in Japan, where feelings are more important than concepts, a "clash of skins"—that is, when two people do not get along with each other—is a far more serious matter than a clash of ideologies. Hori Shigeru, former secretary-general of Japan's ruling Liberal Democratic Party, was quoted in the *Asahi Journal* of 1 September 1976 as saying in defense of his party's apparent lack of a conceptual framework:

> Our party was not brought together by some theory or ideology. It is founded on such things as direct human contact and affection for the organization. . . . We derive our unity from the warm feelings we have for each other. Isn't it better to arrive at a concensus by talking things out if you can?

This helps to explain why litigation is avoided in Japan, why in the United States there are more than three hundred thousand lawyers for a population of a little more than two hundred million while in Japan there are only twelve hundred for a population of about half the size. Human relationships in Japan are not based on ideology or law; they are dependent, in the words of Hori Shigeru, on "direct human contact" and "talking things out." But we must be careful not to misunderstand these terms. "Talking things out," for instance, does not mean a dialectical process of theoretical argumentation, as the term might imply in the West. It is more likely simply to refer to a "gathering together," for the Japanese are not a particularly talkative people.

The most important thing in a society that prizes concreteness in human relationships is to maintain direct physical human contact as much as possible. Not surprisingly, therefore, entertainment expenses make up a significant proportion of the budget on an individual, corporate, or even public level. Even before the war a survey in 1926–27 showed that while the average Japanese white-collar worker spent 3.2 percent of his disposable income on his children's education, he spent nearly three times that, 8.3 percent, on entertainment expenses. In those days too, it took more money to maintain direct personal contact with those important to you than to educate your children.

Since the war, corporate entertainment expenses have been tax deductible up to a certain level, and in 1979 they were estimated to have totaled some $12 billion, an amount comparable to the gross national product of many nations! Furthermore, the Japanese are always holding meetings or conferences, and hotels do a huge business in catering for banquets. Indeed, this is the land that holds some 2,400 festivals a year throughout the country, and the land where the average working person attends five or six year-end parties annually.

For all that can be achieved by mail, over the telephones, by facsimile, or through on-line bank machines, people still end up running around a great deal, for anything short of personal, "skin-to-skin" contact is less than satisfactory. No fewer than 230 sixteen-car bullet trains ply the 500 or so kilometers between Tokyo and Osaka, further evidence of the importance of person-to-person contact even in this age of telecommunications. But this is to be expected. The tradition of gathering together goes way back beyond the tea ceremony into the mythical age of the gods, when deities too favored get-togethers. Moses was alone when he received the Ten Commandments from Jehovah, but according to Japanese mythology, Japan's first laws were promulgated after a heavenly conference of eight million gods had talked over matters. Even today tradition holds that for one month of the year, the tenth month, all the gods, feeling the need to reaffirm their bonds, gather at Izumo Shrine in Shimane Prefecture. This is why the tenth month is popularly called "the month without gods."

Although the Japanese hate to be alone, they also do not like to be in large groups, intimate contact not being possible among large groups of people. The history of tea gatherings confirms this. Hideyoshi used to hold large outdoor tea parties to which huge numbers of people would be invited. But this gradually gave way to gatherings of ever smaller scale until finally four-and-a-half mats was adopted as the spatial standard and five or six people came to be considered the ideal number.

The five-person group was a traditional means of organizing rural and urban citizens during the Edo period (1603–1868). Benedict, too, discussed how small groups were the cornerstone of Japan's modernization, noting that in 1930, fifty-three percent of all people engaged in factory work were employed by "pygmy factories" and home industries having five workers or fewer.

Professor Nakane Chie has stated that "sociologically speaking, in Japan the concept of individuality resides at the small group level," and that "the ideal size for small groups is between five and seven people." We will discuss this matter in more detail later, but the point here is that the small, intimate tea gathering—a product of the reductive consciousness—represents the ideal group size at the work place and in Japanese society itself. Yet we must bear in mind that this small-group system did not come about consciously; people did not decide deliberately to reduce the size of the basic groups in which they functioned. Rather, it was a gradual and natural process, and produced a group size where intimate contact was possible.

The Concept of the Theater

"Gathering together," which reduces the space between human beings to the point where physical contact is inevitable, is called in tea ceremony *ichiza konryū* (literally, "putting up the box seats"). The term implies creating a theatrical performance revolving around the interaction between host and guests. This theater is a physical place and the actions that occur there, as well as a performance in which host and guest—or performer and audience—strive to harmonize their feelings.

It might help to think of it in terms of magnetism. When people meet in their everyday life, they are like ordinary iron with no magnetic field established between them. But in the tea room, a mysterious magnetic power draws them together, which is why all activities there are governed by a set of rules that differ from the principles that guide people in their daily lives. The tea room, therefore, is a theater of human relationships in which host and guest become one.

Westerners have long looked with an uneasy eye on the almost magnetic cohesion found in Japanese groups. This apprehension surfaced in the "yellow peril" theory aimed at the supposed threat posed by Japanese cohesion and the sheer number of the Chinese. In more recent times it can be found in the Japan, Inc. concept, which has Japanese industry, government, and people working together to flood the world market with exports. But Japanese cohesion has long been misinterpreted. The term "Japan, Inc.," for example, is misleading. It simply reflects the contractual, profit-oriented bias of the West. But Japan's groupism and cohesion are different. If we analyze them, we see that they are not something handed down from the upper echelons of the corporation but are in fact rooted in the theater of tea ceremony. Rather than saying "Japan, Inc.," we should be saying "the Japan Theater," and rather than "economic animal," "dramatic animal."

This helps to explain how the Japanese go about unifying subject and object through "performance."

To begin with, in order to achieve complete harmony between host and guest at a tea ceremony, all must become actors. The host must play the host by being solicitous of his guests and formally preparing and serving them tea. The guests must play guests by showing respect and gratitude to the host, drinking the tea, admiring the utensils, and making all the appropriate comments at the right time.

It is interesting to note that through the influence of Nōami many of the movements in tea ceremony were derived from those of Nō actors on the stage. This further underlines the sense of tea as a performance. As in the theater, each action is executed according to a script. It is by involving both host and guest in a single drama that unity between them is achieved, and distinctions between them abolished. In the tea ceremony, this is known as *cha-sanmai*, "an unfettered mind through tea" (*sanmai*, which is rendered here as "an unfettered mind," is the Japanese equivalent of the Sanskrit term *samadhi*, used to describe the mind at complete rest, perfectly concentrated, and allowing of no distractions). Yet the drama of tea is different from drama on stage, the latter being essentially founded on deception (for example, the scenery is a re-creation of reality) whereas the former is quite real; the guests actually do drink tea.

Crucial to the drama of the tea ceremony is the fact that the tea the guests drink is made for them before their eyes. In the earliest forms of tea ceremony, before the tea room was developed, specially trained retainers made the tea in a separate room, then brought it in to the host and guests, who drank it together. This kind of tea party can be found almost anywhere, in Korea, China, or the West. But eventually this process was made peculiarly Japanese by preparing and drinking the tea in the same room, and the tea ceremony was born.

In this way the guests can appreciate the host's sincerity and generosity by actually watching the way he prepares the tea. And the host can directly experience the guests' gratitude by their respectful drinking of the tea in his presence. A one-sided giving or one-sided receiving would not really produce a meaningful relationship between host and guests. But in the tea ceremony the host and guests perform together in an organic and harmonious theater.

In the world of tea there is an admonition, "Don't just make tea for people," which means the host should not just make tea for his guests simply because he has nothing better to do. It is not unlike telling a violinist, "Don't just play music for people." Playing the violin is not like offering someone a chair. The violinist does perform for the pleasure of others, but that is not the only reason. He also performs for the joy and satisfaction he derives from it. Similarly, with the tea ceremony it is not only the taste of the tea but the participation of the guests as well that makes for a successful performance.

The tea master Kobori Enshū was referring precisely to this when he discussed the formal meal that often accompanies the tea ceremony:

> Even if you serve but one dish, it will be enough so long as you do so with good will. On the other hand, you might serve any number of dishes—sweet trout caught from the river rapids, carp pulled up from the depths— but there is no reason to expect that the food will have any flavor at all if you serve it carelessly and without sincerity. Do not let the woven fence or the path in your garden become choked with vines or the guests will never come, drawn by the sound of your kettle softly hissing like wind through the pines.

Preparing food in front of the guests who are going to eat it gives them the added pleasure of a visible demonstration of the host's thoughtfulness. For in Japan, the trouble the host has gone to in preparing the meal is even more important, and more appreciated, than the taste of the food.

After a meal, a Korean or Western guest will thank the host or hostess by saying that the food was delicious. But the Japanese use the expression *gochisōsama deshita*, which literally means: "You (the host) have run around frantically (preparing the meal)." It is an expression of gratitude that acknowledges not so much the end result as the process, that is, the time and trouble the cook put into preparing the food. Indeed, the closer we look at Japanese cooking the more we see that the process is emphasized over the taste.

It is often said that Japanese cooking is to be eaten with the eyes. As Roland Barthes put it: "The Japanese food tray is like an exquisite painting." The small bowls and dishes, and the food on them, form a multicolored abstract painting. This is particularly true of the formal meal that sometimes accompanies the tea ceremony. White soup in a red lacquered bowl, colorful fish paste cut to shapes in accord with the season, a trout arranged to look as though it were leaping through the clear rapids of a stream—all are a feast for the eyes.

I must confess that I sometimes hesitate to actually eat a Japanese meal. I feel like a barbarian destroying a beautiful work of art. I have even, on occasion, felt a little indignation at being faced with such a lovely creation, one that will disappear in a moment like an ice sculpture in the sun. Yet I wonder if we are not missing something if we dwell only on the pictorial beauty of Japanese cooking. The fact is that the exquisite arrangement and delicate coloring of food on a Japanese tray are an indication of the cook's sincerity and concern. The food is presented to the guest like the first lines of a linked verse which the guest will then cap. If we look at it this way, it is clear that the beauty of the food is just a means to allow the host and guest to create an artistic performance together.

Japanese restaurants are different from their counterparts in China, Korea, and the West in at least one important respect, and that is that the cutting board is brought right out in front of the guests. Generally speaking, food preparation in other countries proceeds on the other side of the wall, and the guest only sees the finished product. The cutting board is not something one would take outside the kitchen. However, the Japanese cook wields his knife right under the eyes of his customers. Kyoto's *yūsoku* cooking is the most dramatic example of this: the cook brings out the cutting board, cuts the fish, arranges it, and serves it to the guest off the board itself.

The cutting board represents the process of food preparation, and another word for cook or chef in Japanese is *itamae*, "the one in front of the board." That is why even if they are not actually prepared in front of the guests, *sushi* and whole seafood carved while still alive are often served on a cutting board instead of a plate. In this way the cutting board becomes the center of a cooking and eating performance in which both host and guest participate. Even that favorite among Westerners, *sukiyaki*, is cooked in the presence of customers or guests. The onions, the thinly sliced beef, and the other ingredients are cut and arranged beforehand on a plate which is then brought out to the customers. Then all is cooked while the customers watch. The same applies to everyday Japanese eating habits, to such ordinary actions as dishing out rice. While Koreans bring out the bowl already heaped with rice, Japanese fill the rice bowls one at a time as needed and at the table. Even in the family, the "host" and "guest" participate together in the drama of mealtime.

Like the "theater of tea" and the "theater of cooking," Nō and Kabuki are dramatic forms in which the actor (host) and audience (guests) are united. In other stage forms, the actors rearrange or change their costumes backstage where the audience cannot see them. On the Nō stage, however, there is a special area, in full view of the audience, where the principal actor will have his costume changed or rearranged in the middle of the performance. In certain plays he even puts on or takes off his mask there.

The construction of the Nō stage also serves to enhance the sense of actor and audience uniting in the creation of a theatrical event. Jutting out into the audience, the stage can be viewed from either the front or the side, thereby making it inseparable from the audience. Another difference between the Nō stage and Western stages is the *hashigakari*, an open, bridgelike runway that leads from backstage right onto the stage itself. This allows the audience to watch the entire entrance or exit as a process and contrasts with the usual Western practice of assembling actors on the stage before raising the curtain, or killing the lights at the end of an act so that the spectators cannot see the actors exit.

Emphasis on the process of creating a performance is even more pronounced in the Bunraku puppet theater. In puppet theaters elsewhere in the world, the puppeteer manipulates his doll with "invisible" strings or other hidden devices and tries to stay out of sight himself. But in Bunraku the puppeteers, though usually hooded in black, are there on the stage showing their technique to the audience, puppeteers and puppets working together to stage a performance.

But more than any other performing art it is Kabuki that most clearly demonstrates an approach to theater which seeks to replace the giving and passive receiving of a performance with a communion between actor and audience. Perhaps the most unusual feature of the Kabuki theater, and surely one that is unique to Japan, is the *hanamichi* (literally, "flower path"), a runway that stretches from the back of the theater, through the audience and up to the stage. It acts as both an extension of the stage and an extension of the audience, and as actors come and go on it they are brought in close contact with the spectators. When actors make their entrance along the *hanamichi*, they inevitably stop at a certain spot for a moment. In the old days actors would receive gifts (*hana*; homophonous with the word "flower") from their admirers while standing on the *hanamichi*, and this is how it got its name.

The *hanamichi* allows many kinds of interaction between actors and audience. For example, in one play a character who is sitting on the runway tosses a scrap of paper into the audience. In the past, spectators used to fight over that bit of paper just as people do nowadays when a home run is hit into the stands. Another play, *Imoseyama*, features two *hanamichi*, one on the left and one on the right. The plot involves two lovers separated by a river, and each runway represents a bank of the river. The two characters talk back and forth across the audience/river. When a scene is well played on the runway, the distinction between performer and spectators dissolves.

Even literature, which one would surely have thought was an individualistic art form, is brought into the metaphoric theater of Japanese life in the form of linked verse (*renga*). Though it is true that Chinese or Korean poets would sometimes gather and compose poems together, with each poet adding his or her verse link, this was looked on more as a game than as serious literature. Other forms of linked literature in these countries, for example capping older poems or continuing them in a more contemporary vein, were usually the work of a single writer. However, in Japan, solo efforts were the exception, and linked verse was almost by definition a group performance.

In the West one writer would imitate another probably for the purposes of parody, thus producing not a communal "theater" but a kind of "antitheater." Think of Baudelaire's prayer: "Please let me compose just one verse, one beautiful verse, that will prove that I'm not like the rest of those fools." Poetry is looked on as a statement of one's own existence. Yet in Japan even poetry is made the product of teamwork.

Like the tea ceremony, linked verse is written, or performed, in a Japanese-style room with a flower arrangement on the ceremonial shelf and a scroll on the wall. And while tea has a host and guests, in a linked verse meeting one member acts as a kind of leader. He begins the poetry sequence by offering the opening verse, just as the host at a tea ceremony offers a cup of tea. Tea ceremony guests drink in turn, and, likewise, the poets at a linked verse meeting compose their verses in turn. When a hundred verses have been written, a title is affixed to the sequence and the meeting is over. Furthermore, the composition of verses is as strictly regulated as are the actions in the tea ceremony.

It is not surprising that the performances of tea and linked verse should be so similar since both arose in the Muromachi period (1336–1568). At that time competitions in both tea and verse were popular. People were awarded points for the tea or the verse they had prepared, and prizes were given. Gradually the competitive aspects of these activities disappeared, and both became performances in which all parties cooperated to create art.

Individuality is detrimental to linked verse. Since everyone is working together, the first verse is of the utmost importance for it must be one that the other poets can build from. And although each verse thereafter is composed individually, the rules of linking mean that by definition any single verse will be influenced by the one before it and will in turn influence the one following.

The same thoughts apply to linked *haiku* verse (*haikai*), a later form of *renga* popular among *haiku* poets, as a famous story about Bashō and one of his disciples, Kyorai, illustrates. The two were invited to compose linked *haiku* with a certain Masahide, who acted as host. Masahide asked Kyorai to provide the opening verse, but the latter could not come up with one, so Bashō composed it. The host capped this, and then it was Kyorai's turn. This time Bashō did not like the verse he supplied, and proceedings were halted until it had been corrected. After the session was over, Bashō scolded the hapless Kyorai for the rest of the night. The critic Yamamoto Kenkichi comments that "it was through this kind of training in the performance of *haikai* that the members of Bashō's school became assimilated into the group."

It was not so much that Bashō was convinced he was a poetic genius qualified to lead as that he wanted his students to learn how to fit into a group of poets so as to create the best possible linked verse performance. This is why he lamented the state of linked *haiku* verse with the poem:

No one left
To walk this road
As autumn's evening falls.

Yamamoto Kenkichi sums it up: "Bashō was searching for a new poetic elegance, and a new kind of group performance."

The Hanamichi in Modern Society

The reductive concept of "theater" can also be found in the Japan of today, in the cooperative associations and festivals that bind a village together, and in the management of large industries. Be it among producers and consumers, sellers and buyers, those who provide information and those who receive it, "theater," that complex relationship between host and guest that we have been discussing, is everywhere in evidence.

One of the best places to find this "theater" is in the *depāto*, that particularly Japanese manifestation of the common department store. Here we find uniformed employees repeating "Welcome!" thousands, no, tens of thousands of times a day. The department store hosts special art exhibitions, and Japanese use it as a place to meet friends and have a meal together. In the elevator, even though information regarding what is sold on every floor is clearly posted both inside and outside, the young woman operator repeats all of the information at each stop. Clearly the department store is no ordinary market, but a wonderful theater of buyer and seller.

In fact, this sort of theater occurs in any store in Japan. Whenever you hand over money for something you are buying, the clerk will accept it and say, "I am taking X-many yen." Then, when he hands back the change, he will state the amount. If there is no change, he will say, "I am taking the exact amount." At first glance this might seem to be an overly cautious, if not meaningless, practice, but in fact it is part of the script for good seller/buyer relations. This solicitude takes even more extreme forms. For example, when a small shop closes for a day, the owners are more than likely to put up a sign on the door reading, "It is truly selfish of us, but we hope you will allow us this day off." Can people still be saying things like this, you might wonder. But this unique Japanese sense of performance is as much a part of modern daily life as it is of the traditional arts. Nothing could illustrate this better than the station platform, a place most people see several times a day. Here, it is not just the eyes that are struck; the ears too are subjected to a constant bombardment, both on the platform and inside the train itself. Countless words greet the eye, endless pronouncements fill the air. Not advertising, but the constant information, warnings, even demands that the station personnel are trying to convey to the commuters.

There is no end to it. First there is the door of the train. The public address system warns us: "Take care not to let your hand get caught in the door." Inside the train you are told: "Since this train may have to make sudden stops, please hold on to a strap or handrail." Between stations the conductor will announce the name of the next station, and he is also liable to add some appropriate greeting such as "Good morning!" or "You must be tired after a long day." Then comes a whole catalogue of warnings and instructions: "There's a gap between the train and the platform, so please watch your step," "The door is about to close," and "The train is about to leave." Sometimes you even hear, "Please ensure before alighting that you have left nothing behind on the racks." Furthermore, before the doors close, bells ring and buzzers buzz by way of warning—all this on top of the announcements!

Now let's take a look at the platform itself. In addition to signs indicating where the doors will be when the train pulls in, there are notices from the stationmaster proclaiming, "Don't run onto the train—it's dangerous!" and "The platform gets very crowded at the bottom of the stairs, so please pass on down." Another sign—somewhat superfluous, you might say—reads: "Please be careful because the platform is narrow here." And more and more announcements, most of them ignored, such as: "People carrying skis should be careful because the ceiling is low here," "The next train has just left the previous station," and "At the next station the doors will open on the left side of the train." But if people ignore them—and with so many announcements this is inevitable—why bother in the first place? Why? But of course, to create a "theater" of cooperation between those who run the train and those who ride in it. In London or Paris or New York, running trains and riding them are separate matters. But in Tokyo the train station platform is like a nursery playground where the station personnel take good care of their charges.

If an excess of announcements is largely innocuous, the same cannot always be said of the custom of pushing people onto the trains. In order to keep the trains running efficiently on the admirable web of railways that covers Japan, the stations hire part-time help, usually college students, to join their own personnel in squeezing passengers into the crowded trains during the rush hours. A certain amount of shoving is perhaps inevitable, but in Japan people are hired expressly for that purpose. In Seoul the overcrowding on public transport is even worse than in Japan. People may be pressed into service as "shovers," but it is only as a temporary expedient; no one does it as a job.

Aizawa Masao has the following to say about the history of the "shovers" in Japan:

> On 29 September 1955 the head of the National Railway system announced at a press conference that henceforth trains would no longer be permitted to leave the station with doors partly open. Instead, three hundred students would be hired part-time at fifty-four stations throughout the city to make sure all passengers were securely inside the trains before departure. . . . And on 24 October of that same year the first "shovers" made their appearance on the platforms of Tokyo's Shinjuku Station. [From *Nippon daiichigō kiroku hyakunenshi* (*One Hundred Years of Firsts in Japan*), Tokyo: Kōdansha, 1981.]

"Leaving the station with doors partly open" refers to the practice of having the train pull out exactly on time whether or not all the passengers are safely on board and regardless of whether arms, legs, coats, purses and the like might be caught in a partially closed door. This was not deemed conducive to good conveyor/passenger "theater," so the decision was made that it would be preferable to help pack as many people as possible safely into the train.

As we have seen in the tea room, packing people together makes for good relationships in Japan; in fact it is one of the basic principles for the "theater" of human relations. Although National Railway rules forbid the use of "excessive force" on the passengers, clearly the demands of the "theater" often take precedence.

Assembling Things

There is more to the tea ceremony than just the gathering together of guests for tea. It also involves the collecting of tea ceremony utensils. Thus in tea, the relationship between people and things is as important as that between people and people.

The poet and Zen priest Seigan Shōtetsu (1381–1459) touched on the tea customs of his day in his book *Shōtetsu monogatari* (*Shōtetsu's Tales*): "The true tea enthusiast is one who collects, fusses over, and cherishes tea utensils—bowls, kettles, water jars—to his heart's content." The same could be said of golfers in modern Japan, whose perfervid pursuit of exactly the right clothes and equipment lays them open to the charge of being nothing more than "rich duffers." Indeed, it would be no exaggeration to say that the essence of tea ceremony lies more in the utensils used than in the actual drinking of the tea and that Japan's unusual approach to tea arose precisely because of the Japanese curiosity about and fondness for "things" and their penchant for collecting them. Tea utensils have shaped the history and spirit of tea as much as anything else.

Already in the earliest days of tea gatherings people were using teabowls imported from Tang China, and even today a bowl once favored by a famous tea master remains of inestimable value.

This tradition helps to explain the modern Japanese penchant for designer brands—it has to be a Gucci bag, Lodenstock eye-glasses, a Dupont lighter, a Dunhill pipe.

We discussed earlier how feeling takes precedence over principle in Japan. For the Japanese, who prefer things reduced to a concrete form rather than vague, expansive abstractions, it is quite natural to think and communicate in terms of "things," or objects. Thus when Shukō set about revolutionizing tea, he "declared" his intentions by changing the kinds of utensils used for tea ceremony. He replaced the colorful, highly decorated Tang Chinese ceramics with much simpler Japanese wares from the kilns of Bizen and Shigaraki.

One thing, however, remained unchanged: the practice of using for the tea ceremony objects that had not been specifically designed for tea. Just as earlier tea masters had favored Chinese medicine jars and the like for their tea gatherings, so Shukō and those who came after him made use of farmers' salt jars or fishermen's baskets. Their choice of such utensils redefined the spirit of tea. Later masters like Shōō and Rikyū also based their refinements of the tea ceremony on the utensils they chose. Their ideal was summed up in the phrase "keeping a prize horse in a grass hut," and this further encouraged tea enthusiasts to collect fine pieces.

So circuitous are the histories of famous tea utensils that even the most skillful Japanese storyteller would have difficulty condensing them into a few lines. There is the Ido teabowl called *Kizaemon*, whose owner was so reluctant to part with it that he wore it hanging from his neck when he went into battle, where it was found when he was eventually killed. The Chinese-style tea caddy named *Hatsuhana* (*First Flower*) has a history that reveals the ebb and flow of politics in the Momoyama period (1568–1603): first it was owned by Ashikaga Yoshimasa, then by Oda Nobunaga, then by Tokugawa Ieyasu; within a month it had passed from Ieyasu to Hideyoshi, then to Ieyasu again.

The enthusiasm of certain Japanese for tea had disastrous consequences for Korea. Hideyoshi's fondness for Korean pottery was certainly one of the reasons he launched his invasions of Korea in the 1590s. In fact, these invasions have been called "the Pottery Wars" by the Japanese themselves. Korean celadon perfectly matched the tea ceremony aesthetic: its shapes were often irregular, its surface unrefined, even rustic. The bowls from which Korean farmers ate their rice or soup were treated by Japanese tea connoisseurs as treasures of unparalleled value, and this contributed to their support for the invasion.

Hideyoshi's favorite was a cylindrical Korean celadon teabowl, to which an interesting anecdote is attached. One day, Hideyoshi's page dropped the bowl and broke it. Hideyoshi was about to have the youth executed, but a senior retainer persuaded him to spare the boy. The bowl itself, which is still in existence, was entrusted to Sen no Rikyū, whose repair work was so skillful that the bowl, its crack clearly visible, looked even more suitable for tea than before. Indeed, some people suggest that Hideyoshi might even have planned the whole affair as a bit of theater to enhance the value of the piece.

In fact, the tea master Furuta Oribe, one of Rikyū's students, actually did break teabowls that he deemed too perfect. He would then repair them by filling the cracks with gold or lacquer. An unbroken teabowl had no character; the pleasure was derived from the chic effect of repairing the cracks in a way that would create a striking color combination. This reminds one of the "happening art" of the 1960s.

The Japanese love for "things" stems from more than just a sense of practicality. Take for example the bamboo spoon (*chashaku*) used in tea ceremony. There is very little to distinguish it from a piece of broken-off bamboo, but there was a time when tea scoops were made of ivory. This strip of cut bamboo is naturally of a shape suitable for scooping tea, so it is left as it is with no added decoration or design. In spite of all this, the people who made the spoons would sign them, and the spoons themselves are treated as objects of great value, indicative of the refinement and spirit of the tea master who produced them.

There is an interesting story regarding the bamboo spoon known as *Tama-arare* (*Hailstone*). In the midst of a battle, Furuta Oribe noticed a section of bamboo in his shield that he thought would make a perfect spoon. He began to whittle it down on the spot, and so absorbed did he become in his task that he forgot all about the battle and was only reminded of what was going on around him when a bullet lodged itself in his leg. Sen no Rikyū, it is said, spent his last moments on earth carving a bamboo spoon. When at last he finished, he committed ritual suicide at the command of his fickle master, Hideyoshi. Apocryphal though it may be, this story tells us a great deal about how Japanese regard the relationship between people and things.

The same sanctity is attached to utensils for the tea ceremony as to a rock, a tree, or a mountain. If "gathering together" of people is the first principle of tea ceremony, then assembling the utensils is the second.

The host at a tea ceremony is like a priest. It is his duty to assemble and respectfully lay out the "ritual" utensils. The guests are like worshipers who have come to pay their respects to the sacred objects. A guest must follow a prescribed ritual when he enters the tea room. First he goes to the ceremonial shelf to admire the scroll and the flower arrangement there. Then he examines the hearth, the kettle, the water jar, and so on. Drinking the tea itself is a way of appreciating the teabowl. The host signals the end of the ceremony by placing the bamboo spoon on the lid of the tea caddy and putting the lid back on the water jar. At precisely this moment, the guest of honor asks for permission to look more closely at the tea caddy and spoon, and all the guests in turn admire them. In other words, the tea ceremony both begins and ends with an inspection of the "things" used in it.

In the assembling of the utensils, as in the gathering together of the guests, we see the reduction process in action.

As with the tea master and his utensils, so with the soldier and the pistol that he carried with him in the Second World War. It was decorated with the chrysanthemum crest of the imperial family. More than just a weapon, it was a concrete symbol of the soldier's loyalty to the throne, his martial spirit, and his commitment to the war effort. The formal receiving of the gun and its proper use took on almost mythical significance. The gun he carried was a concrete representation of all he was willing to die for.

Japanese reverence for objects can be seen in the way Western civilization has been assimilated. Christianity—unlike in Korea, for example—has made few inroads. But the tangible products of the Western outlook have been grabbed, treasured, and transformed. Japanese tourists take this attachment to "things" with them when they go abroad. Of course, there are those who are curious about another country's history, customs, the way its people live or what they think. But all that most Japanese tourists want to do is go shopping. It is not so much sheer acquisitiveness as the feeling that by buying something made in that country they can purchase an understanding of its culture. This is why the custom of buying souvenirs for the folks back home is so strong in Japan. The souvenirs are seen as a way of learning about the area that produced them. And bringing back something for loved ones is a way of telling them without words all about the trip.

Another manifestation of Japanese reverence for objects is provided by the national itch to rush out and buy the latest gadget. This is why the Japanese are so susceptible to any sales pitch that includes the expression "just put on the market" (*shinhatsubai*). Market researchers claim there are some four hundred thousand impulsive buyers in Japan, people who will run out and purchase anything new so long as it seems novel and practical. According to another unusual set of figures, there are as many homes that are not connected to sewers as homes that have electronic organs, twenty percent in each case.

The "gathering together" tradition of the tea ceremony reveals itself nowadays in another unlikely form, the propensity in Japan to buy things in sets. Even that most important of choices, marriage, involves sets, the bride being expected to contribute a specified set of goods to her new household. In the early 1960s this set consisted of three items: a chest of drawers, a commode, and a dresser. Later a storage box and a Japanese-style dresser were added to the list. Nowadays a color television, refrigerator, electric fan, vacuum cleaner, and electric rice cooker might be included. Department stores actually sell sets of these things to prospective brides. It reminds one of the Three Sacred Treasures—the mirror, the sword, and the jewel—that have been the symbols of the Japanese imperial family since the time of the first emperor.

The Japanese love to measure standards of living by reducing things to sets of three. After the war it was a refrigerator, an electric fan, and a television. In the early 1970s one had to have the three C's: car, (air) conditioner, and color television. The elegant gentleman is expected to have an English suit, a Swiss watch, and a French lighter. And the three treasures of the upper middle class are French bread, brandy, and drip coffee.

5

REDUCTIONISM TODAY

Transistors Reflecting the Japanese Spirit

When Japanese discuss the spirit of the age in the years just before and after the Meiji Restoration (1868), they are likely to relate the following episode concerning Sakamoto Ryōma (1835–67), folk hero and supporter of the imperial cause.

Once Ryōma spied his fellow loyalist Higaki Naoharu, well known for his skill as a swordsman, swaggering down the street. The latter was sporting a long sword, popular among young people at that time. Ryōma said to him, "From now on, most of the fighting is going to be indoors, so a short sword would really be more useful." And he showed Higaki the one he himself was carrying. The younger man soon switched to a short sword himself and showed it to Ryōma when next the two met. This time Ryōma said nothing; instead, he pulled a pistol out of his pocket and shot it off into the air. Several months later the two ran into each other again, and Higaki proudly showed off his new pistol. Ryōma just smiled and pulled a book out of his pocket. "That gun is old hat now," he said. "From now on *this* is what will rule the world." It was a book about international law.

What if Ryōma had been alive a hundred years later, after the Second World War? "From now on *this* is what will make the world move." And out would have come something the size of a packet of cigarettes: a transistor radio!

In 1955, Japanese were for the first time able to listen to that national institution, the All-Japan High School Baseball Championships, while walking down the street, sitting in a bus, or eating at a restaurant. The transistor radio was born. But probably most of the fans were so absorbed in the games they were hearing that they did not realize the transistor radio itself was Japan's come-from-behind, game-winning home run. In February of that year, the forerunner of the Sony Corporation put out the first transistor radio, the TR 55. It was soon to become the first "made-in-Japan" item to overwhelm world markets since the folding fan. But the transistor was not invented in Japan. It was originally developed in the United States, and the first transistor radios in Japan were made with transistors supplied by Western Electric. Why is it, then, that we associate them with Japan?

History holds the answer, in the form of the fan, that first great adopted import of a thousand years ago. It was the Japanese, not the Americans, who thought to expand the transistor's use, to bring it into the hands of the people and make it a marketable item. Japan—the country where people used to build collapsible boats that could be carried around in a box, the country where people "shrink" huge trees down to tiny bonsai, the country where people pack lunches into boxes. It is natural that the transistor too should flourish there. Within two years of the development of the first transistor radio, Sony had come out with an even smaller model, the TR 62, the world's smallest, so small that it could fit in the pocket.

We must not forget here that even before the transistor radio was developed, there was already a boom in the manufacture of radios. At the end of the war, all that was left in Japan were ashes and millions of repatriated soldiers. The factories were in ruins. Food, energy, and raw materials were in desperately short supply. Radios were among the few products that could be easily manufactured.

People often say that Japan's economy depends on its ability to export to world markets, but this I think is a misrepresentation. Whenever Japanese industry puts out a new product, the first to buy it are Japanese consumers. It is normally the case that only if it succeeds on the domestic market do companies mount an overseas sales campaign. The Japanese consumers, with their love for things small and handy, are the arbiters of what will succeed overseas.

The tactics that Sony, standard-bearer of the transistor revolution, used were the tactics of reductionism. The company describes itself in the following terms in its publicity: "To make things smaller yet retain high quality, to make things that are interesting and useful—that is the Sony spirit." That is the spirit of reductionism, and, in a way, the spirit of Japan itself.

My point becomes clearer if we look at the history of the Sony Corporation. Sony's first product was not the transistor radio but a tape recorder. Having heard German magnetic tape recordings, the president of Sony, Morita Akio, brought out in January of 1950 the first tape recorder to be produced in East Asia. Unfortunately, it weighed about forty-five kilograms and was very expensive, since the tapes had to be coated by hand. Needless to say, it did not sell very well.

But Morita applied the Japanese spirit to this Western technology. He shut his R and D staff up in a hotel with orders to make that tape recorder smaller and cheaper. And they did. They came up with a model that could be carried around like a suitcase and cost about half the price. In later years, using methods based on the same approach, they developed the world's smallest stereo and the world's lightest headphones, and now we have the Sony Walkman portable stereo. In the 1980s, competition in the field of home electronics is a competition to see who can make the smallest and handiest product. And this is where the Americans and Europeans lose out to the Japanese. About the only area where their rivals have an advantage over the Japanese is in the manufacture of large appliances like refrigerators that cannot be carried around.

Video cassette recorders present the same story. They were first invented in the United States in 1951 at the Bing Crosby Laboratory. In 1957 they were first used in commercial broadcasting by CBS. And it was Philips, not a Japanese company, that simplified the equipment for home use. But the companies that further reduced the equipment in size and developed the means to put an entire movie on a single small cassette were Japanese companies. Sony and Victor Japan jumped into an early lead and seized between them ninety percent of the world market. Since then, Sony has made its video equipment even smaller and has come out with the world's first magnetic video camera which dispenses with film.

Sony and Victor are far from being the only Japanese electronics firm to have done this sort of thing. Numerous other companies have succeeded in making their products shorter, smaller, lighter, and thinner, which is why Akihabara, the center for Tokyo's retail electrical trade, is a showcase of worldwide state-of-the-art electronics.

A commercial for Sharp, the company that first developed the electronic calculator, sheds more light on the situation: "When Sharp put out the world's first electronic calculator in 1963, it was the answer to our dream of making the computer accessible to anyone." Not only was it Sharp's dream, but it was the dream of all Japanese. While Americans may have dreamed of inventing the computer, Japanese dreamed of shrinking it down and putting it in everyone's home. If the American ideal is invention, the Japanese ideal is innovation.

That reduction is a hallmark of Japanese electronics should come as little surprise if we recall our discussion of the rock garden in Muromachi Japan. The essence of rock gardening aesthetics was summed up in the words of the garden designer Tessen Sōki: "A thousand miles is shrunk down to one foot."

The Japanese dream led from the desk-top calculator to the wrist-watch calculator, and now we are in the age of the microcomputer. At the heart of this reduction technology is the ever smaller circuit.

If Ryōma were alive today he would be busier than ever. If his friend got hold of a transistor, he would have to pull out an integrated circuit. And as soon as his friend got his hands on an IC, Ryōma would have to come up with an LSI, and then a VLSI, with a hundred thousand or a million transistorized circuits on a single silicon chip measuring five millimeters square. Not for nothing is Kyushu called "silicon island" and the rest of Japan "the silicon archipelago."

Nowadays articles about microcomputers appear alongside the pictures of nude women in weekly magazines, and newspapers are full of advertising and information on them. Lectures are delivered about them on television, and bookstore displays feature "how to" books on them. Computer classes are offered in every neighborhood. And as of 1979 it was estimated there were some 910,000 Japanese who worked with computers as a leisure activity.

That little giant, the VLSI, is today's Issun Bōshi. Now the Japanese are trying to join him to machinery in a new field called "mechatronics" (a word which itself is a Japanese coinage). The Japanese have a lot riding on this tiny silicon giant, for here is a country where *mikan* oranges and hot springs are often said to be the only natural resources, where fifty-five percent of the food and eighty-nine percent of the energy is imported. Japan is forced to turn to high value-added industries to offset its import costs.

Reductionism and Management

In the field of automobiles, too, reductionism has paid off. Small Japanese cars have wrested the number-one spot from the American auto industry. One of the most successful Japanese cars on the American market has been the Toyota Crown. Into its compact body the manufacturers put power windows and, somehow, doors solid enough to bang shut with a sound like that of a Cadillac. The German Volkswagen company simply makes small cars, but Japanese cars are large automobiles reduced in scale, and surely that is what accounts principally for their popularity.

Cameras and watches, too, show the Japanese talent for making small, portable items. Significantly, the companies that produce these reduced-scale goods themselves apply reductionism in their management. As Sony's Ibuka Masaru has said:

> I'm not at all tempted to try and make our company one of those giants with huge amounts of capital. There is merit in small scale. For one thing, we can be more responsive to change. A big company would not have that flexibility.

And indeed Sony is a relatively small company. Rather than dissipate its resources, it is able to pick one area and throw all its people and money into that area. Sony's president Morita likens the company to a destroyer that is able to maneuver freely. While in most other countries people believe that bigger is stronger, the Japanese prefer the smaller alternative. That is why, although the bigger companies are better known, it is the smaller ones that are more representative of Japanese industry.

Japanese history, too, shows that the major changes were almost always brought about by small groups with a single purpose in mind. As Shiba Ryōtarō points out in his dialogues with Donald Keene, the impetus for the Meiji Restoration came from Japan's smaller fiefs. Intellectual pioneers like the progressive thinker Nishi Amane (1829–97) and the writer Mori Ōgai (1862–1922), for example, came from the relatively minor Tsuwano fief in Iwami province (present-day Shimane Prefecture). And the saying used to go, "To study Dutch [i.e., Western] learning, go to Uwajima," a small domain in the west of Shikoku.

Things have not changed. Nowadays, too, enthusiasm and new ideas seem still to come from smaller groups. According to Professor Yasuda Hisaaki of Tokyo Electrical Engineering College, Japan's current status in the field of personal computers "owes little to the brains gathered together at the famous research laboratories and just as little to the large-scale research projects with vast amounts of funding." It was, for example, a relatively small company, Mabuchi, that developed a motor of positively Lilliputian size now used in electric razors, tape recorders, and all sorts of other goods. It took a little company to develop a little motor that has proved invaluable in the home.

The basis of Japan's modernization was in "pygmy factories" of just five or six workers. The policy adopted by the Occupation forces of breaking up the *zaibatsu*, the huge business conglomerates, and forbidding any single company to employ more than a hundred workers actually had a salutary effect on Japan's economic recovery. Although the policy was short-lived, it bolstered Japan's latent reductionist approach to management.

As a company grows bigger, it gets more and more abstract, and direct human contact becomes more difficult to maintain. As a result, a marked tendency has arisen among large Japanese companies to spawn "child companies." Sometimes these child companies outdo their parent companies, as when Victor Japan, an offshoot of Matsushita Electric, developed the VHS video cassette. Mammoth though it may be, there are many ways in which Matsushita itself resembles a medium- or small-sized company. In its style of management, for example. This is brought out by Richard T. Pascale and Anthony G. Athos in their book *The Art of Japanese Management*. They note that top members of the management either meet directly with or talk by phone to those responsible for each work section, and visit the work site or factory and meet with customers directly.

The various well-known features of the Japanese management landscape—lifetime employment, participation decision-making, and centralized employment practices—all boil down to one thing: a cooperative performance between employer and employees. This is seen most dramatically every morning when, at precisely eight o'clock, all eighty-seven thousand Matsushita employees join together to sing the company song, as though to make all employees one. New members of the company are given a thorough indoctrination in the Matsushita philosophy, and every employee in the company must give a five-minute speech in front of his or her work group about the relationship between Matsushita and society at large.

This may appear totalitarian, or perhaps reminiscent of the militaristic Japan of the 1930s, but there is a big difference: here the "host" and "guest" choose to merge together rather than relate in a one-sided way. The modern employee has a uniform that distinguishes him from outsiders, just as the samurai had their family crests, the merchants their shop curtains, and the artisans their short jackets. And it is not just a matter of the employee sacrificing his individuality for the benefit of the group. Members of management, in a sense, sacrifice their group identification for the individual by becoming involved in special occasions like the marriage of an employee—something that Americans would probably consider an invasion of privacy.

This point is elaborated on in a comparative study of Matsushita Electric's Kōnosuke Matsushita and ITT's Harold Geneen, made by the writers of *The Art of Japanese Management* (New York: Simon & Schuster, 1981):

> One can see clearly the great difference between Mr. Matsushita and Mr. Geneen in the ways they "thought" about human beings in reference to the subject/object dichotomy. Geneen seemed to regard other people as objects to be used to achieve his purpose, while Matsushita seemed to regard them as both objects to be used and subjects to be honored in achieving his and their pur-

poses. When Geneen found an executive wanting, the man was humiliated or fired. When Matsushita made a similar discovery, the man's group was marked as ineffective and he was reassigned, even demoted, and the opportunity for the individual to grow from the experience was stressed.

To translate these comments into the terms I have been using, it is through "theater" that Japanese management seeks to resolve the adversary relationship between labor and management that has been the plague of capitalism. This approach has been an important factor in Japan's economic success.

The "theater" of producer and consumer, however, is no less important. Pascale and Athos note in *The Art of Japanese Management* that "the most important aspect of the Matsushita sales 'system' is the zealous personal attention Matsushita gives to the customer." They quote Matsushita on the subject: "Our social mission as a manufacturer is only realized when products reach, are used by, and satisfy the customer. . . . It is therefore vital for an enterprise to have the quickest possible information on what the customer is asking for. We need to take the customer's skin temperature daily."

Matsushita is not alone. Most other companies demonstrate their concern for their customers by their emphasis on complete, almost intrusive, after-service. So successful has Japanese industry been in establishing a cooperative theater with consumers that Japan has produced no Ralph Nader nor large, American-style consumer movements.

The Robot and Pachinko
The Japanese extend their proclivity for "theater" to the world of machines. They have none of that Western dread of the mechanical intruder so humorously portrayed by Charlie Chaplin in *Modern Times*. For one thing, Japan's lifetime employment

system makes it highly unlikely that a worker would actually find himself without a job as a result of a robot. Furthermore, Japanese factories operate on a rotation system, with workers moving from job to job. Thus if a robot takes over a human job, the worker is simply shifted elsewhere. Therefore, mechanization in Japan produces no dramatic displacements such as occurred when the steamship replaced the ferryman or when the mill replaced the waterwheel. To the extent that the robot relieves people of tedious, dirty, or dangerous work it is welcome, and it now exists in such numbers in Japan—over fifteen thousand, more than in any other country—that there is clearly no going back.

There are, inevitably, people in various walks of life in Japan who fear robots will have a damaging impact on employment, but few people who actually work on the shop-floor have complaints. They know that if they are moved away from production they will be absorbed into the ever expanding service department. In a sense, Japan is entering an age where the robot heroes of children's comic books are coming to life.

All this is true and has often been stated, but far more important is the Japanese tradition of creating a cooperative "theater" between people and the utensils they use. In the old days, when writing brushes or tea whisks wore out, people would ceremoniously bury them as a gesture of gratitude for the service they had rendered. Surely this kind of "theater" stands behind Japan's ability to exploit the robot so successfully.

The economist Takeuchi Hiroshi maintains that the Japanese actually treat their robots with love. He notes: "At Nissan Motors' Zama plant, robots are called by the names of beautiful actresses and entertainers. This tells us a great deal about how Japanese workers regard robots on the assembly line." He even goes so far as to say that, "having given the robots endearing nicknames, the workers seem to work together with them as though they were human co-workers." Because the workers treat their robots like people, they keep them in good operating order, fix them when they are out of kilter, and generally go to a great deal of trouble for them. Workers at the Fujitsu Fanuc factory, Japan's largest fully automated plant, also give names to their robots, although they prefer commoner names than those chosen by the Nissan workers, names like Tarō (a popular Japanese boy's name), Sakura (cherry), and Ayame (iris).

In the West, "things" are objects to be used. In monist Japan, however, thoughts and feelings are attributed to things. Things become an end in themselves rather than a means to an end. For instance, when guns were first introduced into Japan, people were more interested in decorating the handles than in making them more effective killing instruments.

The theater of Japanese life, extended in this way to the world of machines and to the factory shop-floor, finds another startling outlet in the pinball game called *pachinko*. The popularity of *pachinko* surely has to be counted one of Japan's stranger phenomena. As a leisure activity, *pachinko* ranks third in popularity, behind drinking and cards, with an estimated twenty-five million people playing annually, according to a study compiled in 1979. *Pachinko* outstrips mah-jongg and *shōgi* (a form of chess) in adherents, suggesting that many people would rather play games with a machine than with human partners.

Fads tend to be very pronounced in Japan, but *pachinko* is an exception. Although the game is supposed to have been invented in Detroit in 1910, it never really caught on anywhere until it came to Japan in about 1935, where it became an immediate and immense success. To all intents and purposes, therefore, it is a Japanese game. From the time it was introduced in Japan it has never known an off year. It immediately spread to all parts of the country and at one time 315 *pachinko* parlors were built in the space of half a year in Kōchi, a smallish city in southern Shikoku. An article in the *Ōsaka Mainichi* newspaper of the time described the phenomenon as it was in its early years:

When the doors open at 7:00 A.M. the customers are already there waiting impatiently. Wherever you go, the parlors are completely full. At closing time no one shows the slightest inclination to leave, so the employees have to turn off the lights and chase everyone out. The profits are so phenomenal that the owner and employees can afford to be arrogant.

The type of *pachinko* machine we know today did not appear until after the war. The first of the postwar machines was called "Little Thing," and the machines have been evolving ever since. *Pachinko*'s popularity has continued unabated, and it now has an annual turnover of eight billion dollars. It is so lucrative that the town of Kiryu in Gunma Prefecture switched over from producing textiles to manufacturing *pachinko* machines and now makes sixty thousand of them a year, half of Japan's total output. Of course, *pachinko* machines too have entered the electronic age. Their insides are crammed with integrated circuitry, and they are a far cry from the simple machines they once were.

If someone who knew nothing about the game took a peek inside a *pachinko* parlor, he would probably think it was a factory of some sort. The machines, constantly emitting electronic noises, are lined up in banks, and the aisles in between are barely wide enough to pass through. The people sitting motionless in front of the machines and staring at them fixedly look for all the world like women in a spinning factory or researchers performing some delicate experiment that requires complete concentration. It is hard to believe these people are at play, not work.

The customers are totally absorbed in turning the handle with just the right amount of pressure to shoot little steel balls (eleven millimeters in diameter) through a thicket of nails and into slots that will reward them with more little balls. This is the crystallization of the reduction process: people packed in a small place, in direct physical contact with machines, staring intently at the little balls and the tiny nails, the atmosphere tense with anticipation.

The teahouse used to be an urban retreat. In this industrial age it seems that city dwellers prefer to hide out in crowded *pachinko* halls. They have not a glance for the people to the right or left of them. Nor do they hear the stirring marches that blare out over the sound system. And the incessant, deafening rattle of balls that overwhelms the entire place goes absolutely unnoticed. It is just one person facing one machine, a dialogue with little steel balls.

But what would happen if suddenly everybody except that one person got up and left and the martial music and background racket suddenly ceased? Of course, it would cease to be *pachinko*, for while *pachinko* may look like an individual pastime, it needs the whole cacophonous, gaudy background of noise and color to sustain it. Only in the context of that noisy, crowded, frantic atmosphere does it become a true retreat where the average Japanese can shut himself off from social pressures and condense the whole of his conscious being into communion with a machine. Thus this modern urban retreat, the *pachinko* parlor, represents in its own way the reduction principle at work in the society of today.

Speculation and Innovation

The former president of Sony Corporation, Ibuka Masaru, expressed this opinion on the difference between Japanese and American electronics:

> In the American electronics industry advances are usually the result of research undertaken for the purposes of defense or space exploration. In Japan it is quite the reverse. All of our technological advances stem from our effort to make goods that will suit the needs of consumers. [*Asahi Shinbun* newspaper, 2 August 1981.]

American discoveries are prompted by the expansive, the abstract—that is to say, space exploration and weaponry. Japanese electronics, however, is oriented toward the consumer and the small parlor in which everyday life is lived. In short, we could call this the difference between "expansion electronics" and "reduction electronics."

The space shuttle, that explorer of outer space, is clearly a product of American technology and the American outlook. Sixty-five percent of the component parts of *Himawari*, Japan's weather satellite, were made in the United States. The culture of the United States, a nation that is willing to explore the unknown, is a culture of speculation and inquiry. Japan's, on the other hand, is a culture of assimilation and innovation. The motto for American culture is "maybe"; for Japanese culture it is *naruhodo*, "now I see."

Rabelais's last words are supposed to have been: "Now I am off to look for the Great Maybe. I wonder if it will be in a magpie's nest. Well, ring down the curtain. The play is over." Faulkner's works are full of this same sense of potential. In the short story "Race at Dawn," a hunter named Ernest has finally caught up with a deer he has been chasing, but he lets it go. Surely he is speaking for Faulkner when he says: "Maybe. . . . The best word in our language, the best of all. That's what mankind keeps going on: maybe." It was for this "maybe" that the first settlers crossed the Atlantic and later moved ever westward in their covered wagons. And it was for this "maybe" that cowboys herded cattle across the vast plains. America owes its expansive outlook to the pioneers and cowboys. Armed with this attitude of inquiry and speculation, people can conquer the unknown and make new discoveries.

The Japanese, on the other hand, have always been motivated by a desire to assimilate and innovate. Not for them this challenging the unknown. Their strength lies in recognizing and understanding what already exists. They function within the realm of the possible. Japan has taken so much from other lands, first

China and Korea, later Europe, and since the war the United States. It has always borrowed well-established aspects of existing societies, things that have proven to be possible. Then it assimilates, innovates, and refashions them into something Japanese. Nor is this something new. The Japanese have been doing it for centuries. Within half a year of seeing their first gun, brought to Japan by the Portuguese in the mid 1500s, the Japanese had applied the "now I see" approach and produced six hundred guns of their own. Within some ten years they had made over thirty thousand, more than Portugal itself possessed.

Private Japanese research laboratories have been accused of being more interested in collecting information and developing other people's technology than in doing any original scientific research of their own. And it is true that the ratio of original technology exported to original technology imported is one to five. But these "now-I-see laboratories" take the technology they have imported and the information they have gathered, improve on it, then turn around and export products that surpass the originals.

Matsushita Electric is one of the best practitioners of this "now I see" approach. Its strategy, put in baseball terms, is to bat second. From the very start, Matsushita has emphasized quality and price over new technology. Thus it has developed few new products of its own, preferring to make other company's products for less, and backing them up with excellent marketing. A good example of this is the video tape recorder. Just as Sony pursued and overtook Philips, so Matsushita pursued and has overtaken Sony. It succeeded in capturing the market by making the product smaller, coming out with longer-playing tapes, and developing a cheaper VTR system. Analyze your competitors' goods and find out how to make them better—this is Matsushita's approach, and this is the approach of Japanese industry.

Like Matsushita, so Mitsubishi. Makino Akira, vice-president of Mitsubishi Research Institute, maintains that Japan's national character is not particularly suited to hitting home runs in the field of new technology. "Japan," he says, "industrializes the technology that its developers could not raise properly. This suits our national character perfectly."

In the Japanese martial arts, the strategy is to use your opponent's own strength against him. This manifests itself in many aspects of Japanese life. For example, the distinctive curve of Japanese castle walls served to strengthen the walls by absorbing and redistributing the outward and downward pressure of the earth packed inside rather than simply trying to contain it. Certain rock groupings in Japanese gardens perform the same function. In other words, the "now I see" culture, the culture of assimilation and innovation, needs an opponent in order to work most effectively, and it needs someone in front of it to take the lead.

Ever since the Meiji Restoration of 1868, Japan has been trying to pursue and overtake Western civilization. In 1952, after the Occupation forces had left and Japan was on its own again, the country's gross national product ranked lower than that of such nations as Chile and Malaysia. Yet by 1967 it had overtaken Italy, and in the following year, the hundredth anniversary of the Meiji Restoration, it passed one of its own mentors, Britain. In the same year, it was the turn of France, and in the following year West Germany. Now, in terms of GNP, Japan really is batting second. In the 1980s, the road is wide open for Japan.

Until now, Western civilization has been oriented toward increases in scale and size, in administration, in industrial life, and in the plans, aspirations, and ambitions of individuals and nations. Recently, however, things have changed. As E. F. Schumacher has suggested in his book *Small is Beautiful*, the age of "giantism" is over.

Japan, with its tradition of smaller is better, its rejection of ideology, its sensitivity to information, is perfectly positioned to take the lead in the coming age of reductionism. It has been a thousand years since Sei Shōnagon wrote, "all things small, no matter what they are, all things small are beautiful." How ironic that we should now be hearing the same refrain from the other side of the Pacific!

EXPANSIONISM
AND THE JAPAN OF TODAY

Pulling in Other Lands

Enough of the present. According to a Japanese myth, in ancient times the deity of Izumo (today's Shimane Prefecture), Yatsu-kamizuomitsu no Mikoto, dissatisfied that his own realm was so small, gazed across the sea at the Korean peninsula and the continent beyond and cried out: "Too much land. I see too much land." So he cut off part of the continent and pulled it over to Japan with a net. Then he sewed it onto Izumo province. This myth, which is believed to refer to the migration of people from the peninsula to island Japan, illustrates that primordial Japanese inclination to haul in what is outside rather than expand outward themselves. As we have seen, nature, the moon, the gods were all drawn into the Japanese home. Foreign culture has been treated the same way.

Even though they are surrounded on four sides by the sea, the Japanese have never been a seafaring people. They have, for example, neglected the stars. Stars are of vital importance to anyone who wishes to sail, which is why Greek mythology is full of deities associated with stars. But one looks in vain for a star deity in Japanese mythology. And although the *Man'yōshū* poetry collection describes many natural phenomena, very few of its thousands of poems even mention stars. What has been called the world's first astronomical observatory was built in Korea in the seventh century. But the Japanese did not even know stars moved, they did not even recognize the existence of the North

Star until the early seventeenth century.

When the inward-looking Japanese, who value things close to them, things they can touch, go out into the great, wide world, their consciousness and their very behavior change. Look what happened when they took to sea in the fifteenth century—they became pirates. But these pirates were, after all, Japanese. They could not really adjust to foreign lands. At one point they wrested an island from the Chinese, but after three months they abandoned it and withdrew.

This is where the two Japanese concepts of "inside" (*uchi*) and "outside" (*soto*) enter the picture. "Inside" is the reduced and concrete world that one knows from direct experience. "Outside" is the abstract world of expansion. The Japanese have a tendency to divide everything they come into contact with into either "inside" or "outside" and act accordingly.

"Inside" refers to oneself, one's family, and one's home. Indeed, the Japanese word *uchi* can mean either "inside" or "house," although now different Chinese characters are used to distinguish the two words. Anything beyond the home is "outside." As we saw earlier, the Japanese are a fastidious people who cannot bear the sight of dirt. So they sweep and wipe and clean to rid their homes of dirt. But what is outside is another matter. People are not quite so fussy about dirt in the office as they are about it in their own home. But compared to society as a whole, the company is "inside," so they are more concerned about the cleanliness of, say, the desk at the office than about how the outside world looks. That is why you are likely to see cigarette butts and litter on platforms in Japanese train stations. On the other hand, compared with nature outside, one's own city is "inside," which explains why you see even more litter strewn about on mountain trails. And so it goes on. Compared to the rest of the world, Japan itself is "inside," and as a result domestic tourists in Japan are better behaved than are Japanese tour groups abroad. It seems the further Japanese go "outside" the more they lose of their

Japanese characteristics. In fact, the expression "throw away all sense of shame when you are traveling" shows that ethics for "inside" and those for "outside" are perceived to be different.

This difference is clearly defined. The Japanese have a genius for small, "inside" gardens, but large public parks are anathema to them. There is a refined beauty to the ceremonial shelf in a private home, but Japanese cities lack any overall sense of balance or beauty. The same Japanese who are unfailingly sensitive to the chirping of tiny insects, remain totally unrattled by the incessant din spewed forth from loudspeakers in public places. Surely there are no other people in the world who would tolerate the racket raised by politicians giving speeches from trucks with loudspeakers blaring. The same dichotomy exists in attitudes toward the sights of the country. As Edward Seidensticker has pointed out, the Japanese take such good care of their man-made gardens, even designating them National Treasures, while at the same time heedlessly despoiling such beautiful natural scenery as that of the Inland Sea.

The Japanese sense of "inside" and "outside" works like boxes-within-boxes. Indeed, it calls to mind a Japanese castle. First there is the inner castle enclosure, beyond that the second and third enclosures, and beyond them the gate to the outside world. The inner enclosure is the smallest and most tightly packed. As you move out from there the sense of reduction becomes less and less pronounced. Naturally, people feel most secure "inside" the inner enclosure. Friendships are like this. Your friend becomes part of you (*miuchi*, in Japanese, which literally means "inside the body"), and together you will help each other through the vast flow of life.

Traditional organization of villages reflects this too. Several households would gather together and build their homes within a single walled enclosure. Clusters of these homes would make up a village. Thus the village formed a greater "inside," while at the same time the individual groups were an "inside-within-an-inside" where people treated each other like members of the same family. Even in modern cities, there are district councils and neighborhood associations formed on a voluntary basis. According to the Ministry of Home Affairs, as of November 1980, there were 274,700 of these councils throughout Japan.

During the Edo period (1603–1868), ten events were designated as involving group cooperation: birth, coming of age, marriage, death, memorial services for the dead, fire, flood, sickness, setting off on a journey, and building work. If a particular person did something bad or harmful to the village well-being, cooperation would be denied him for eight of the above (only in the event of death or fire would people help him). This gave rise to the term *mura hachibu*, literally "eight tenths of the village," which nowadays has come to mean "ostracism." This and disinheritance essentially mean chasing out someone who is on the "inside." To the extent that people on the "inside" are close to each other, their feelings of exclusiveness toward those on the "outside" are that much stronger. In this sense, foreigners in Japan are always ostracized to some degree.

This is substantiated by a story from the world of Japanese professional baseball. As related by Robert Whiting in his book about baseball in Japan, *The Chrysanthemum and the Bat*, in 1965 two players were battling it out for the Pacific League home run title. One was an American named Spencer, who was playing for the Hankyū Braves, and the other was the famous Japanese catcher Nomura Katsuya, who at that time was playing for the Nankai Hawks. As the race between them got tighter, the pitcher in one game deliberately walked Spencer. When the latter protested, he was told, "Why should we let a foreigner take the title? If we (the pitchers) are to give the title to anybody, why not give it to Nomura?" Such is the logic of "inside" and "outside." Incidentally, Nomura went on to win the title that year and become the first player in the history of Japanese pro baseball to win the triple crown.

There is a certain humor to this story, but other examples are not so funny. For instance, there have been thirty-three movies made depicting the suffering of Japanese victims of the atomic bombing of Hiroshima, but none of them dwell on the many Koreans who were also killed or injured in that tragedy. For that matter, there is as yet not even an accurate count of the Korean victims, and they have frequently been denied the medical care that is offered other victims by the Japanese government. These Koreans are in fact victims twice over, for they were forcibly removed from their homeland in the first place and put to work in Japan. That only one Japanese, Sakari Zenkichi, will stand up and testify on behalf of Korean victims of the atomic bomb shows how sharp the division is in Japan between "inside" and "outside."

Even Japanese, once rejected from the group, are treated like foreigners. The lone wolf is an outsider, condemned to live on the edge of starvation. In France, if someone is called "different," it is usually an expression of praise. But in Japan the term is used to label someone who does not fit in the group, someone who is to be ostracized. The further Japanese get from the group, the more they lose their sense of existence. And if they go to some foreign country, which is as far "outside" as they can be, they become completely different people, "not like the guy I used to know." This is why we find a type of crime among Japanese abroad that is virtually unheard of in Japan itself. There was, for example, the model company employee, transferred to South America, who shot a local child to death while the latter was picking up golf balls. There was the Japanese living in Greece who, angered when his dog was run over, beat an innocent bystander to death with a rock. And there was the Japanese graduate student, in Paris working on his dissertation, who carved up his girlfriend and ate her.

The "outside," it seems, poses challenges that the Japanese are ill-equipped to meet. They lapse so often into what I think of as the three S's. There is the Silence of Japanese members at an international conference, the Smile of those who react to anything that is said with a broad, but vague grin, and there are the ones who Sleep through meetings.

Japan has had great difficulty establishing a foreign policy that other countries consider coherent. It has often been criticized for being only concerned about its own national welfare. For example, at the time of the 1973 oil embargo, Japan was quick—far too quick, some thought—to repudiate its relations with Israel and establish friendly ties with the Arab nations. When the rest of the world was condemning Rhodesia's segregation policies, Japan raised not a squeak—not, that is, until the African nations organized a boycott and Japan's own economy was directly affected. Again, when the Japanese Red Army hijacked an airplane to Bangladesh in 1977, the Japanese government showed not the least concern for the rest of the world but simply followed its own interests in acceding to the hijackers' demands. However skillful the Japanese may be at creating cooperative "theater" within their own country, somehow when they get on the international stage they are less successful.

The criticism is often heard that while Japan is a member of the world economic community, when it comes to trade in other senses it is as isolated as it ever was. The Japanese still do not seem to be a part of the global village, nor do they seem to be as concerned about being ostracized from that village as they do about being ostracized from one of their own villages.

Why is it, then, that of the various manifestations of Japanese culture, only manufactured goods succeed so well in the world of expansion? There is a little irony in the answer to that—the last secret of the reduction culture. The folding fan and the box lunch were products of the reduction impulse of their age, but as soon as they were made they expanded outward precisely because they were convenient and easy to carry. What makes the folding fan work is the principle of reductionism, but because it was functional it sold well on the world market. In other words, as soon as reductionism manifests itself in a functional object, it becomes expansive. The same Japanese that developed the delicate, lovely folding fan turned around and became pirates in order to market it. Japanese history is full of such paradoxes.

The Samurai Merchant

The Japanese reduction impulse produced the transistor and the semiconductor, and Japanese sales techniques had them appearing in shops throughout the world—very much an expansionist process. This paradox has in turn produced the current trade friction. No matter how many countries they surpass economically, the Japanese remain isolated from the international community, stubbornly clinging to their "inside" versus "outside" mentality. In this sense, only their bodies are adult, the rest is child. They are in danger of becoming stunted Issun Bōshis.

The West and the rest of Asia eye Japan suspiciously. Do the Japanese have any sense of international responsibility, they ask themselves, or are they trapped in Village Japan? Does Japanese culture have anything to contribute or is it only dedicated to profit for Japan? These doubts have given rise to such pejoratives as "economic animal." It is widely acknowledged now that Japan can no longer live by inward-looking logic. Reduction has served to turn Japan into an economic power, but now it poses a serious threat to the country. Inside Japan, this reductionism produces objects of great beauty and value. But on the world stage Japanese diligence prompts the epithet "worker bees," Japanese concentration appears as "naked ambition to overwhelm the world marketplace," and creating cooperative theater seems like nothing more than a policy of exclusion.

A cartoon in a Western newspaper once depicted a Japanese, wearing a medieval warrior's helmet and carrying a sword at his side, roaring around on his Honda motorcycle. The rest of the page consisted of an advertisement for price cuts on automobiles and in bold black letters the catch phrase, "The Japanese made us do it!" In 1970 *Time* magazine took Japan to task by comparing today's overseas Japanese salesman to the "warrior trader of the 14th century" and the "soldier bureaucrat" of the Second World War. "The difference," it said, "is that the latter-day *wakō* carries a *soroban* (abacus) instead of a sword and wears blue serge instead of the khaki of General Hideki Tojo's Imperial Army."

Fierce Japanese competition has, for instance, crippled the motorcycle industry in several countries. In Britain, it is now defunct. In the United States, high tariffs exist to protect the machines of Harley-Davidson. And in Italy, more stringent measures still have been adopted to keep the domestic industry viable. The motorcycle industry represents perhaps the most extreme example. But severe dislocation has occurred in many Western industries as a result of Japanese competition. In May of 1981, the German camera maker Rolex filed suit against Japanese camera companies for patent infringement. The German mass media took up the call, claiming that their prized industry had fallen before the Japanese onslaught. The following month, the Swiss company SSIH, makers of Omega watches, announced the layoff of all of its employees, as it had fallen hopelessly into the red. As recently as 1975, it had been the world's number-one watch manufacturer, producing sixty-nine million units a year. But then the Japanese digital watch typhoon struck, and gone was the symbol of Switzerland. Singer, for years a company synonymous with the words "sewing machine," was so hard pressed by Japanese competition that it was forced to close its Elizabeth plant in Scotland, a factory that had operated for over one hundred years.

A different sort of problem has arisen over the approach the Japanese adopt toward contracts. Again, within a Japanese context, the possibility of misunderstanding has been minimal, but when contracts have been struck with foreign corporations, a different outlook has occasionally led to serious strain. One of the most famous cases involves a beef export contract signed by Japan and Australia in 1974. At the time Japan was faced with a shortage of beef, so a trade delegation was quickly dispatched to Australia to ask the Australians to increase exports to Japan. At first the Australians refused, fearing that it would cause the price of domestic beef to rise and thus hamper the government's fight against inflation. Eventually, however, an agreement was reached. In order to fulfill it, the Australians increased their production of beef, but meanwhile the Japanese shortage had turned to a surplus. Japanese beef producers started exerting pressure to stop imports, so Japan unilaterally abrogated the agreement. And thus did Australian beef dance to Japan's tune. Korea has had similar trade problems with Japan. To give just one of many examples, although Japan runs a three billion dollar annual trade surplus with Korea, Korean fishermen cannot export their seaweed to Japan because of Japanese restrictions.

Japan's critics, especially in Europe, have tried recently to steer discussion away from the arid ground of trade statistics. They argue that to the extent that trade issues affect employment, they are a political issue as well. Rancor has also been caused in Europe by what is perceived as a Japanese reluctance to tackle problems until the storm has burst, at which point hasty remedial measures are cobbled together. The Japanese response to this line of thinking has been voiced by a high-ranking official of the Ministry of International Trade and Industry in unusually outspoken terms:

> Europe woke up in the morning to find that the Rising-Sun flag had been raised overnight in the area which it regards as its own traditional sphere of influence . . . its own "Greater Europe Co-Prosperity Sphere." . . . Japan's competitive power is overwhelmingly great. If we compare it to a golf match, Japan's handicap is single

while that of Europe is 25 or 26. [Quoted from Endy-mion Wilkinson, *Misunderstanding: Europe vs. Japan*, Tokyo: Chūō Kōron Sha, 1981.]

Other developed countries have asked: if Japan's power to compete is so "immense," why does it appear so consistently to be trying to hold down the newly industrialized countries? The Japanese Foreign Ministry has publicly announced that Japan will not give Korea any assistance in the field of industrial chemicals, claiming it would prompt a "boomerang effect" (a term the ministry seems to have coined for this occasion) on the Japanese economy. In other words, they are admitting that if newly industrialized countries were given technology, they would use that technology to make goods, then turn around and overwhelm the Japanese market with them. But did the Americans or Europeans complain about "boomerang effects" when Japan itself was a newly industrialized country?

Somehow one gets the feeling one has been down this road before. In the 1930s, Europe and America were hit with an avalanche of Japanese goods. Having crushed Korea and defeated China and Russia at the turn of the century, the Japanese were riding a wave of self-confidence, convinced that they were now one of the great powers, and reductionism gave way to expansionism. The West tried to put a brake on Japanese expansionism. Japanese goods were boycotted, and tariff barriers erected. Japan's patience finally ran out, and it went to war. Now again Japan is abandoning its reductionism and moving toward expansion. The issue now is how the West—and, indeed, Japan itself—will react when Japan once again becomes a great power and seeks to become ever greater.

A Fear of Open Spaces
What happens when the Japanese move hesitantly from the "inside" to the "outside"? We find one sort of answer in *My Nar-*

row Isle, the autobiography of Sumie Mishima. When Mishima entered Wellesley College, her fellow students and friends all treated her very kindly, but she had a hard time nonetheless:

> I did not know how to behave myself in this strange world, and my pride in "perfect manneredness," a universal characteristic of the Japanese, was wounded. I was angry at myself for not knowing how to behave properly here and also at the surroundings which seemed to mock at my past training. Except for this vague but deep-rooted feeling of anger, there was no emotion left in me then. [John Day Company, 1941.]

Mishima observes that the young Chinese women at her school were entirely different:

> What attracted me most in those Chinese girls was their self-composure and sociableness, quite absent in most Japanese girls. These upper-class Chinese girls seemed to me the most urbane creatures on earth, every one of them having a graciousness nearing regal dignity and looking as if they were the true mistresses of the world. Their fearlessness and superb self-composure, not at all disturbed even in this great civilization of machinery and speed, made a great contrast with the timidity and oversensitiveness of the Japanese girls.

Compared to the Chinese, the Japanese awkwardness in coping with the outside world stands out starkly.

Ruth Benedict discusses this same passage in *The Chrysanthemum and the Sword*, noting that "Miss Mishima, like many other Japanese, felt as if she were an expert tennis player entered in a croquet tournament. Her own expertness just didn't count." She goes on to say that this is "the Japanese dilemma of virtue."

But Chinese and Japanese share moral values based on a Confucian outlook. Benedict herself perceives the real issue when she compares the situation to that of a dwarfed, potted pine tree: even though it is a beautiful work of art while it stands in a small garden, if you transplanted it, it would lose its beauty and charm.

Toyotomi Hideyoshi, the upstart who united his country and whose dreams of Japanese hegemony in East Asia foundered in the mountains of Korea, provides another, quite different example of Japanese ineptitude when it comes to expansion. In his analysis of Hideyoshi, the critic and historian Kobayashi Hideo maintains that the general "was a splendid hero, yet he was no visionary. But then there is no reason to expect that someone who rose to the top from such low status should be a visionary." Hideyoshi was so confident he could conquer China that he made meticulous plans as to exactly how he would occupy Peking. He promised to make one of his men regent there and talked of bringing the Japanese emperor Go-Yōzei to the Chinese capital. He even ordered exhaustive studies of just what ceremonies such an imperial visit would entail.

So why did he fail, given all that planning? Why, in spite of his skills as a tactician, all his battle experience, and his successes in diplomacy, did Hideyoshi not even manage to get as far as Pusan, let alone Peking? Kobayashi suggests it was because Hideyoshi misunderstood the region he was dealing with, and notes that the general's men were astounded at how large Korea was. One of his aides wrote back, exasperated: "Oh! But this country is big! Much bigger than Japan, I would say." In fact, of course, Korea is no such thing. But the Japanese troops, taken away from their "inside" and set down in the unfamiliar "outside," saw only a great, unfathomable vastness, and this inability to size up the unknown contributed in no small measure to their eventual defeat.

The Japanese troops, like Sumie Mishima, found themselves in a situation beyond their grasp, and this proved completely disorienting. The war that everyone thought would be over within a year dragged on for seven. And as Kobayashi points out, Hideyoshi was not only defeated on the battlefield, but he failed in his diplomatic maneuvers with the Ming government in China as well. As successful as he had been in his dealings with Tokugawa Ieyasu, all Hideyoshi could get from the Chinese was a meaningless scrap of paper declaring him "king of the tributary state of Japan."

The ineptitude of Hideyoshi and his men, their inability to deal with the outside world, led to tragedy. The Korean campaign benefited no one, least of all Hideyoshi himself. It seems to me, indeed, that whenever Japan is inward-looking and reductionist it prospers. But having succeeded, it inevitably tries to go too far and ends up embracing expansionism, as Hideyoshi did. And whenever that happens, the Japanese change completely: their sense of subtlety disappears, their capacity for judgment is impaired, and their natural susceptibility to beauty turns to brutality. This is something that Koreans are intensely aware of, for Korea has always been the first victim of Japanese expansion. So it was when modern Japan turned to aggrandizement in the 1890s.

The same lack of judgment, the same inability to function on a large scale that had brought about Hideyoshi's failure, resulted in a Japan reduced to ashes at the end of the Second World War. In Hideyoshi's time, the Japanese had totally underestimated the severity of the Korean winter. Their soldiers had been sent off to fight wearing only sandals to protect their feet. Thousands lost their toes through frostbite, yet they continued to fight wearing sandals. Likewise, in the Second World War the Japanese won a string of early victories using encirclement tactics, but as the war wore on, their tactics wore thin, and they began to lose more and more engagements. Nonetheless, the Japanese clung to their encirclement tactics to the very end, and this contributed greatly to their downfall. The alertness and flexibility of the "attitude" we discussed earlier, which serves the Japanese so well "inside," became single-minded stupidity when transferred to the outside world.

The Handtruck and the Raft

The perils the outside world presents to the reductionist Japanese are well illustrated in "The Handtruck," a short story by Akutagawa Ryūnosuke (1892–1927). Few stories as short as this one have been so widely read and so much loved. Could its popularity have something to do with its exposition in lucid literary terms of that perennial Japanese fear of the "outside"?

One day eight-year-old Ryōhei ventures to the edge of town to watch the workmen with their handtrucks hauling sand and dirt and building materials at a building site. Eventually, his chance comes; he sees two young men pushing one of the trucks, and he offers to help. He helps them push the trolley up through an orchard of *mikan* oranges, and after they reach the top of the hill he hops on for the ride down. Down he coasts, his jacket flapping in the wind, his nose filled with the scent of oranges.

They coast through a bamboo grove, and a forest of trees, then suddenly the chilly ocean opens up wide before them and Ryōhei realizes he has gone too far. They come to a stop and the men go into a tea shop, leaving Ryōhei behind in the truck. He tries kicking the truck, tries pushing it, but it will not move, and he is left all alone as night begins to fall. Finally the young men come out of the shop and tell him that since they are going to stay there for a while he had better hurry home by himself. Bewildered, he runs off in the direction of home. Hungry and frightened, he scurries up the hill, tears springing from his eyes. At last he reaches his village, where everything is just as it should be—streetlights burning brightly, the womenfolk carrying water back from the well, the men returning from the fields. He reaches the gate of his home and, no longer able to control his emotions, bursts into a flood of tears.

Ryōhei's was an adventure in expansionism: riding a truck with strangers into a place beyond his world of every day. Although the handtruck rides along a fixed track, it leads toward the sea, that symbol of expansiveness. At first Ryōhei is exhilarated, letting the wind fill out his jacket like a sail, but once he is left alone and it starts getting dark, he suddenly feels ill-at-ease, and he can think of nothing but getting home as soon as possible. This is, if you like, a story of failed expansionism. It is a quintessentially Japanese story, in length, in tempo, and in emotional scale.

Comparison with a characteristically American story such as Mark Twain's *Adventures of Huckleberry Finn* is, therefore, instructive. In addition to the difference in length, a number of revealing contrasts are to be found. It will be recalled that Huck, who hates the structured life, escapes his village and rides down the great Mississippi River on a raft with the runaway slave Jim. Ryōhei's venture into the outside world takes him no further than the edge of town, from where he can return before the day is out. The handtruck itself is like a rolling box which runs on rails. By comparison, Huck's raft is open-sided, and rather than running on rails, it flows freely along with the wild river. No matter what dangers Huck faces—his raft breaks apart, he is chased and captured—he never thinks of giving up and going home. When Ryōhei gets home he bursts into tears. Huck never cries.

In short, Ryōhei is a child of the reduction culture, while Huck is a child of expansion. In "The Handtruck" we see the limitations of the Japanese when faced with the outside world.

Ah, To Be an Honorary White Man!

Watanabe Shōichi writes in his book *Retorikku no Jidai* (*The Age of Rhetoric*, Tokyo: Diamondosha, 1977):

> He may carry a Dunhill lighter, he may wear Gucci shoes, but the Japanese can never become a white man (nor a black man). He is, and always will be, a yellow man.

Admittedly, this is not a very profound thought, but it deserves consideration nonetheless, not so much for what it says as for the presumption on which it is based. It is only where doubts exist that assertions of this nature are made. No one needs to assert that the sun rises in the east. And in Korea, no intellectual would say something so palpably obvious as "Koreans are not white men, they are yellow." Thus, by asserting that "Japanese cannot become white men," Watanabe is implying he or others believed that Japanese, until now, had the potential to become white men.

Once denied by Westerners the title of "honorary white man" that some had seen fit to give them, the truth dawns on the Japanese that they are Japanese, and that "Japanese cannot become white men." Then the Japanese make an effort to return to the fold, and their previous rejection of the rest of Asia becomes a pan-Asianism. But pan-Asianism is more than just words. After spending all that time aspiring to the position of "honorary whites," then discovering it is all in vain, the Japanese have found themselves shut out of the Asian ambit too. Think of the bat in the fable. He was neither bird nor beast. In the beginning he managed successfully to masquerade as both, but by the end of the day he had been exposed for what he was and rejected by both.

If Watanabe's conclusion is simplistic, so is the idea that by writing books about Japan or sitting in a tea room admiring the garden outside, the Japanese can rediscover their identity. So is the idea that just by sending the Japanese prime minister on a tour of Asian countries, the Japanese can at one stroke write off the past.

For the Japanese nation, as for the greatest Japanese historical heroes, disaster has invariably followed on the heels of success. Japan's neighbors have paid the price, too, the price of Hideyoshi's adventurism, of the subjugation of Korea and Manchuria, and of the Second World War. The seeds of expansionism can be found in a line from the Japanese national anthem, that was especially loved during the time of Japanese militarism: "The tiny pebble grows into a huge boulder." Now the tiny pebble appears to be growing again. The Japanese consciousness is beginning to move outward, and this is something we should watch with care. Japan is often described as an economic superpower. But far more unsettling characterizations are beginning to appear, especially among titles of books both Japanese and foreign. *Japan As Number One, The Emerging Japanese Superstate,* and *Nihon no jidai ga kuru: seiji taikoku e no jōken (Japan's Day Will Come: Conditions for Becoming a Political Superpower)* are among those that spring to mind.

But what would be the point of Japan becoming a superpower? What is to be gained from becoming number one in the world? Why is everyone restless to become so huge? Is the strategy now to outstrip through expansionism that which they have attained through reductionism? Japan should not forget that the big things in traditional Japanese stories were the demons.

An interesting little paper called "Indications of Social Speed," delivered at the 1979 International Symposium on Traffic Safety in Japan, compared the various speeds at which pedestrians walk. The fastest pedestrians in the cities covered were none other than the Japanese. Osaka's pace of 1.67 meters per second was number one in the world. Tokyo was second, at 1.56 meters. Parisians were veritable tortoises, averaging a mere 1.46 meters per second. Even Japan's slowest pedestrians, the people of Kagoshima (1.33 meters), were faster than those of Manila. It is hard to avoid asking the question of where all these people are going in such a hurry.

CONCLUSION:
DON'T BECOME DEMONS,
BECOME ISSUN BŌSHIS!

For our final examination of Japanese reductionism, we go back into the past, to the very beginnings of the story of Japan.

> Now in those days there was a tall tree growing on the west bank of the Tonoki River. In the morning, this tree's shadow fell all the way across the Inland Sea to cover the island of Awaji. In the evening, it fell on Mount Takayasu in Kawachi. The tree was finally cut down to make a boat, and what a fast boat it was! The boat was named *Karano*, and was used morning and evening to bring pure water from Awaji Island. Finally it broke apart, and its timbers were used as fuel for the salt kilns. What was left of the wood after that was fashioned into a zither whose sweet music reverberated to the heavens. [Translated from a modern Japanese-language version by Takeda Yukichi of the *Record of Ancient Matters*, Tokyo: Kadokawa Shoten, 1977.]

To cut down that tall tree and make a boat of it is a kind of reductionism. But reduced as it was, the boat saw people across the wide sea. To burn the wood of the boat and make a zither with what was left over is to reduce even more. Yet the sounds of that zither echoed even further than the boat could ever have gone. The more the tree was reduced, the greater its power of expansion became.

Originally, Japanese culture was huge like that tree on the banks of the Tonoki River. The *haniwa* clay figures found in Japanese tombs of the fourth, fifth, and sixth centuries, the enormous statue of Buddha (the *daibutsu*) at Tōdai Temple, the 120-meter-long building at Izumo Shrine, the tomb of the emperor Nintoku—these are all products of a large-scale outlook. But from the tenth century, the Japanese broke away from continental influence and began to pare things down and reduce them. So at present Japan is in the first stage of reduction: the giant tree made into the boat *Karano*.

However, the Japanese consciousness is still unable to embrace the seven seas. Japan remains at the stage of the *Karano* sailing back and forth to get pure water, only now the "water" is purely financial. They obtain this water with the little giants of reductionism: the transistor, the calculator, the video system, the digital watch, the semiconductor.

In order to advance beyond this stage, the Japanese will have to discover a new kind of reduction, just as the *Karano* had to be burned in order to create the zither. What form that new kind of reduction will take is something our children will find out.

The Japanese now are producing material goods for the world market, but is it not time they exported more of cultural, of spiritual value? Their consciousness is still centered "inside." When they have moved out into the world, with the sword or the abacus, it has been only for themselves. I hope they will try again, but this time with world peace and mutual understanding as their goal. That would indeed be sweet zither music.

Victory by the sword inevitably means bloodshed and someone else's defeat. Victory by the abacus means profits gained at someone's cost and someone's suffering. But victory by that zither, whatever it may turn out to be, would be everyone's gain.

It makes me think of Mother Theresa's words. She said that in the world today there are two belts of hunger, one in Africa and one in Japan. The hunger in Africa is physical, while that in Japan is spiritual.

So, Japan, make a beautiful rock garden that will bring the world together. Create a pure, calm tea ceremony that all people can enjoy. Your history is washed by the blood of samurai warriors, yet from that you redeemed a lovely flower. How sad if you should only be remembered as a brand name on electronic goods. Your success has always been in making things smaller. It is time you moved beyond transistors and semiconductors and found that zither whose sound will be enjoyed throughout the world. The time has come for you to pull off another, more important blow for reduction.

Don't become demons, become Issun Bōshis! Burn that boat and make a zither whose sound will float across the seven seas!

INDEX

Akutagawa Ryūnosuke, 183
Amae, 11, 12, 13, 14
Anatomy of Dependence, The, 10, 15
Arai Hakuseki, 65
Archery, 55, 56

Bashō, 60, 61, 63, 83, 143
Benedict, Ruth, 10, 15, 16, 59, 70, 135, 180
Bentō, 47, 48, 49
Bodhidharma, 118
Bonsai, 24, 87, 88, 89, 90, 91, 95
Bonseki, 88, 89
Box lunches, 47, 48, 49
Bunraku, 141
Busaiku, 20
Business cards, 69, 70
Buson, 63
Butsudan, 106

Capsule hotel, 114
Chanoyu ichie-shū, 127
Chrysanthemum and the Sword, The, 10, 15, 59, 70, 180
"Crawling-in entrance," 116, 117, 122
Crests, 62, 64, 65, 67, 68, 69

Daruma, 44, 118
Dictionaries, concise, 52
Dōgen, 55, 56, 123
Doi Takeo, 10, 11, 12
Dōjinsai, 116
Doll festival, 42

Dolls, 41, 42, 43, 47
anesama, 40, 43, 44, 46, 47, 70
kokeshi, 44
mame, 19

Eisai, 119, 125
Ejima Kiseki, 23
Electronics, 156, 165, 166

Fans, 20, 31–36, 37, 38–39, 77
bat wing, 32
Chinese, 32, 34
cypress, 34, 36, 38
Egyptian, 32
flat, 31, 32, 33, 34, 35, 36, 39
folding, 31, 32–33, 34–36, 37–39, 40, 70, 76, 175, 176
Koryô, 33
Shura, 35

Fencing, 55
Folklore, 18, 19
Furuta Oribe, 149, 150
Fusuma, 39

Gardens, 16, 24, 38, 64, 72, 73, 75–76, 77–87, 88, 89, 92, 93, 94, 118
"borrowed scenery," 75, 76, 79, 80
"contracted scenery," 77, 78–79, 80
rock, 24, 84, 86, 88
Genji Scroll, 64
Gigaku dance mask, 58

Giri ninjō, 15

Haiga, 64
Haikai, 143
Haiku, 20, 21, 27, 31, 35, 36, 37, 60, 63–64, 83, 143
Haji, 15
Hanamichi, 141
Hanten, 67
Harakiri, 130, 131
Hayakawa Shōdō, 92
Hideyoshi. *See* Toyotomi Hideyoshi
Hina matsuri, 42
Hōjōki, 112
Hokusai, 53, 54, 55, 59
Household altar, 105, 106

Ii Naosuke, 127
Ikebana, 55, 91, 92, 93, 94, 95, 129
Ikenobō Senkō, 95
Ikenobō Senmyō, 96
Ikenobō Sen'ō kōden, 93
Ikenobō Sentei, 96
"Inside." *See Uchi*
Ishikawa Takuboku, 25–28, 30
Issa, 21, 37, 62
Issun Bōshi, 18, 19, 21, 24

Japanese language, 30, 31, 44–46
Japanese Society, 10, 15
Jingū, Empress, 32
Judo, 55

Kabuki, 38, 55, 140, 141
Kamidana, 105
Kamo no Chomei, 112, 113
Kanō Eitoku, 51
Kawabata Yasunari, 23
Keigo, 15
Kendō, 55
Kim Sowŏl, 73
Kintarō, 18
Kobayashi Issa, 21, 37, 62
Kobori Enshū, 138

Kojiki, 22, 29
Kokan Shiren, 89
Konparu Zenpō, 129
Kozaiku, 20
Kumi Kunitake, 20
Kyorai, 143

Language, Japanese, 30, 31, 44-46
Linked *haiku* verse, 143
Linked *renga* verse, 142, 143

Mame-emon, 20, 23, 24
Mamesuke, 19
Mametarō, 19
Man'yōshū, 21, 22, 72, 77, 170
Meishi, 69, 70
"Mini-writing Olympics," 41
Miyamoto Musashi, 57
Mizuhara Shūōshi, 64
Momotarō, 18
Murasaki Shikibu, 95
Murata Jukō, 115, 116
Museum of Micro Art, 41

Nakane Chie, 10, 135
Nihonjin no kokoro, 12
Nihon shoki, 80
Nijiriguchi, 116, 117, 122
Niwa. See Gardens
Nō, 38, 54, 55, 59, 96, 129, 136, 140
Nōami, 136
Nō masks, 53, 57, 58, 59

Oda Nobunaga, 48
Ogi. See Fan, folding
Okada Saburō, 22
Okazaki Fumiaki, 79
Ōno Susumu, 22
"Outside." *See Soto*

Pachinko, 163-65
Paperbacks, pocket-sized, 52
Paper lantern, 39

Pillow Book, The, 7, 42, 43, 95
Pocket libraries, 52
Poetry, 25, 26, 27, 28, 29, 30, 31,
35, 36, 37, 60, 61, 62, 63, 73,
142. See also Haikai; Haiku;
Renga
Puppet theater, 141

Renga, 142, 143
Rikyū. See Sen no Rikyū
Ryōkan, 37

Saiku, 19
Sakamoto Ryōma, 153
Sakuteiki, 81, 82, 90
Satō Sadao, 56, 57
Seigan Shōtetsu, 147
Sei Shōnagon, 42, 95
Seiza, 123, 124, 125
Sendenshō, 92, 94
Sen no Rikyū, 92, 96, 116, 117,
148, 149, 150
Senzai hishō, 81
Seppuku, 130, 131
Shakkei. See Gardens, "borrowed
scenery"
Shiga Naoya, 84
Shigetsugu, 35
Shinkokin-shū, 36
Shinto, 105
Shōdō kashinshō, 92
Shōō, 128, 148
Shōtetsu, 147
Shukkei. See Gardens, "contracted
scenery"
Soga no Umako, 77
Soto, 171-74, 176, 179, 181, 184
Sumō, 126
Suzuki, D. T., 60, 61

Tachibana no Toshitsuna, 81, 82,
90, 92

Takeno Jōō, 116
Takuboku. See Ishikawa Takuboku
Tale of Genji, The, 42, 64, 95
Tatami, 113
Tea ceremony, 55, 92, 115–16,
118–22, 123, 125–28, 131, 132,
134–35, 136–38, 142, 147, 148,
149–50, 152
Tea ceremony utentils, 147, 148,
151
Teahouse, 80, 92, 108, 109, 117
Tea masters, 78, 116, 148, 149, 151
Tea rooms, 16, 107, 108, 116–18,
120, 121–22, 123, 124, 125, 128,
132, 136, 137
Teika, 128
Television, 106, 107
Tenji, Emperor, 29
Tessen Sōki, 84
Thirty-six Views of Mt. Fuji, 53
Tokugawa Iemitsu, 129
Toyotomi Hideyoshi, 67, 92, 117,
120, 134, 149, 150, 181, 182
Transistor radios, 24, 40, 153, 154

Uchi, 171-74, 176, 179, 181
Uchiwa. See Fan, flat
Umbrellas, collapsible, 39, 40

Video cassette recorders, 156

Walkman, 155

Yagyū Munenori, 129, 130
Yamaga Sokō, 65
Yamanoue Sōji, 127
Yi Kyubo, 72
Yoshimura Teiji, 73
Yun Sŏndo, 60, 61

Zaibatsu, 159
Zenpō, 129

定価3,500円
in Japan